A Rainbow Book

THE WAY TO AN "A"

HOW TO HELP YOUR CHILD SUCCEED IN SCHOOL

Jan Barrick

RAINBOW BOOKS, INC.

THE WAY TO AN "A"—
How To Help Your Child Succeed In School
by Jan Barrick
Cover Design & Interior Design by Marilyn Ratzlaff
$12.95

Library of Congress Cataloging-in-Publication Data

Barrick, Jan, 1951-
      The way to an "A" : how to help your child succeed in school/
by Jan Barrick.
      p.   cm.
      Includes bibliographical references.
      ISBN 1-56825-009-6 : $12.95
      1. Home and school — United States.   2. Education —
United States — Parent participation. 3. Parent-teacher
relationships — United States. 4. Study skills.
LC225.3.B375   1993
649'.68—dc20   93-26787
                                                           CIP

DEDICATION

This book is dedicated to
Ann Golf Harry,
the Wind Beneath My Wings

ACKNOWLEDGMENTS

To Esther Powell, my fourth grade teacher; she taught me that the average student through hard work, determination, and dedication could excel. She taught me how to study and instilled in me the love of learning. Through her example I learned that teachers must always put the students' best interests first.

I'd like to acknowledge the teachers like Mrs. Powell who put their students first, second, and third. Teachers who understand school rules and policies are important but, when their classroom doors are shut, the students reign supreme.

I'd also like to acknowledge all the teachers who go to school every day to teach students, who put forth unusual effort in order for their students to achieve some degree of success, and whose main goal in the classroom is to instill in each student the love of learning.

SPECIAL THANKS

I am indebted to numerous people who have helped to make this project a reality. I especially owe a great deal of gratitude to my business partner and good friend, Jerry Richardson. His support, patience, and encouragement have enabled me to achieve many of my goals and to make my dream a reality.

I am very grateful to Nancy Young and Steve Findeiss who helped me organize my thoughts and ideas into a very concise, readable book.

I would also like to thank my students and my students' parents. The experience I obtained from working with students and their parents has given me the knowledge needed to write this book.

Jan Barrick

CONTENTS

SECTION III
THE ADMINISTRATIVE WAY
OF MAKING GOOD GRADES . . . 135

INTRODUCTION

When we think of success in school, most people think of good grades. A student's grades determine if he or she will be promoted to the next level in school or will be forced to repeat a year. Ultimately, grades usually determine whether a student will take the technical education path or go to college — in short, the direction of a person's entire career.

On a shorter-term basis, grades can determine whether a talented athlete may participate in Friday night's game or can bar potential leaders from participating in student council and other school affiliated organizations. (Most schools require students to have a minimum grade average in order to participate.)

There are many advantages of making good grades, but in general it can be said that good grades give you alternatives. A student who graduates from high school with a high grade-point average (GPA) can choose from a wide selection of colleges since the first thing college entrance boards look at is a student's GPA. Similarly, the student who graduates from college with a high GPA can usually choose from many competing job offers.

Fortune 500 companies look for college graduates who have high GPA's because, just as the best predictor of how a student will do in college is how he or she did in high school, the best predictor of how a person will perform in a job is how he or she performed in college.

9

Fortunately, students can be taught to make good grades, just as they can be taught to read and write. Of course, there are students who are blessed with a high IQ, and school work comes easily to them. But surprisingly — and fortunately — IQ or inherent ability is NOT the most important ingredient in making good grades.

If having a high IQ is not the most important factor in making good grades, what is? Considerable research shows that the best predictors of student achievement are PARENTAL INVOLVEMENT and family background. When parents become involved in their child's schooling, the child's performance in school improves. The degree of parental involvement determines the degree of success a child will experience.

Accordingly, this book is organized into two main sections. The first section is what parents can do to help their children get better grades. The second section deals with what students can do to improve their performance.

The information in this book has been tested at my centers and in public and private schools. As a typical result, students who enter the program with less than a C average and follow the program exactly usually increase their grades by an AVERAGE of one letter grade in each subject. It is not uncommon to see students' grades literally go from F's to A's.

This program has helped hundreds of students improve their grades. Follow it exactly and you too will soon see your child's grades improve.

SECTION I

WHAT PARENTS CAN DO

WHAT PARENTS CAN DO

The time and energy you invest in your child's education today will enable you and your child to collect the dividends in the future. Everyone has heard that a good education is essential in order for your child to obtain a high standard of living, but you may not realize what a huge difference in average lifetime income a college degree makes: roughly one million dollars over a person's lifetime!

There are other, more immediate benefits to making good grades. Students who make good grades have fewer discipline problems and are less likely to spend time in detention or in the principal's office. When grades go up, self-esteem goes up. Students become more concerned about their appearance. Their peer group often changes. Finally, students who make good grades are much more likely to complete their schooling.

With so much at stake, most people would probably agree that it's worth making an exceptional effort to ensure that their child is part of this group.

Results obtained in my classroom courses show that students can be taught to make good grades just as they can be taught to read and write. In raising students' grades, one factor remains constant: the amount of time and effort your child puts into his or her school work determines how much the student's grades will improve. The same factor holds true with parents: the amount of time and energy you invest, as parents, in your child's education will have a substantial effect on how much your child's grades will improve.

The key here is *unusual effort*. Parents, as well as students, must be willing to put forth unusual effort in order for this plan to work. The rewards will be not only high grades on the report cards, but also children with high self-esteem and self-confidence. Your extra effort will produce students who have developed sound behavior patterns, a work ethic, and the self-discipline that will enable them to succeed in life.

Most parents want their child to do well in school. The problem is that parents often don't know what to do to help their child. That's presumably why you're reading this. So the first thing to do is to determine who is in charge in your home. Are you in charge or is your child? If your child runs the show, this program will probably not work for you.

If you have decided that this is a program that you would like to try, if you have decided that you are willing to put forth the extra effort needed to help your child be successful in school, and if you are in charge of your home, then we first need to discuss the key elements which are necessary to be successful in any endeavor you and your child choose to undertake. Two of the main factors of being successful in anything one undertakes are attitude and motivation.

ATTITUDE + MOTIVATION = SUCCESS

What is success? We usually think of a successful person as someone who is rich or famous. However, there are many forms of success. Success can also mean self-improvement and doing the very best that you possibly can.

What makes people successful? Some people seem to have success in everything they try. They go into each new endeavor expecting to do well. These people have the correct *attitude* for success. With a healthy attitude or approach, to school, business, or any other activity in life, you can improve your performance and find more success. When students have a good attitude, they become more confident. As grades improve, so will their confidence. Confidence in themselves will help them become more capable of other achievements outside the classroom. In school, as in life, attitude will accomplish more than IQ or any natural ability one might have.

Another thing that separates successful people from others is *motivation*. Motivation is the will to succeed, the drive to work toward your goals. (I will discuss goal setting later in this book. See page 28.) Motivation is like the engine of a car that keeps the wheels turning while going up steep hills and covering long distances. The academic journey is long and difficult; parents have the responsibility to keep the motivation well tuned to overcome the obstacles which will come.

You can help your child develop a good attitude and become motivated. Use the following exercises to help you.

Attitude

You may have heard it said that a person who failed at something — a business, a class, a sport — "went into it with the wrong attitude." This generally means that he or she was lazy, badly prepared, or lacked confidence. What is the proper attitude for success? The following brief questionnaire will help you and your child evaluate his or her attitude.

1. How do you feel at the beginning of each day?

_____

_____

_____

2. Do you have specific goals that you are working to achieve? What are they?

_____

_____

_____

3. Do you feel confident that the things you are learning will help you in later life? _____

4. Do you feel confident that you will succeed to some degree at whatever you try? _____

The answers to these questions will tell you a lot about your child's attitude. Encourage your child to approach school work with confidence. Encourage him or her to think about goals for the future. Tell him or her that with hard work and a good attitude he or she can achieve these goals.

Motivation

Strong motivation is important for any effective study program. Motivation is what moves you, what spurs you to work hard, and to make extra effort. Well-motivated students never have to ask themselves why they have to do something. They know what they are working toward, whether it is a personal achievement, a career goal, or the simple satisfaction of learning something new.

Tips on helping students become more motivated:

1. Encourage students to approach school work as something to be mastered rather than a drudgery that has to be done.
2. Encourage students to read about people who are successful in areas in which they are interested or about a career field they hope to enter.
3. Brainstorm ways to make your child's least favorite class more interesting.
4. Help students set their own standards. If an assignment is too easy, suggest additional work to make it more challenging.
5. Help your child think of ways to make school work more fun and less of a drudgery.
6. Parents, PRAISE work well done and REWARD positive behavior!

Summary

A good *attitude* and strong *motivation* are important keys to your child's *success* in school as well as in any other endeavor in life. Good attitudes lead to self-confidence and overall success in life.

Motivation is the driving force that enables students to achieve their goals. Attitude and motivation go hand-in-hand in achieving success.

Encourage your child to set goals for himself or herself outside the classroom. For example, set a goal of making the school football team or getting a part in the school play. Success in activities will bring about a change in behavior patterns.

One of the main goals of this program is to change old behavior patterns and establish new ones that are more conducive to making good grades. Changing behavior patterns is not easy. Structure and consistency are essential to making this program work, and unless you're exceptionally lucky, parents must be the ones who provide these elements.

We'll start the "how to" portion by observing that there are two ways to make good grades. One is obviously the academic way — scoring high on tests and assignments. The other is what might be called the "administrative way" — getting the system to work for your benefit.

Accordingly, the things parents can do to help their children get better grades fall into two general categories:

(1) *academic support,* consisting of things to help your child score better on tests and homework;

(2) what might be called *administrative support,* consisting of techniques you can use to interact with the school system to get the best possible support and effort from the system.

These two categories will be explained in the following sections.

THE PARENTS' ROLE IN ACADEMIC SUPPORT

In developing a strategy for making good grades, it is useful to understand what causes LOW grades. In most schools, the overall grade is determined entirely by scores on homework assignments, test scores, and sometimes a small "nonacademic" component such as attendance. The two main causes of low grades are:

* not turning in assignments;
* making poor scores on assignments and tests.

Both of these problems, in turn, are often caused by a lack of time-management and organizational skills — hardly surprising in children. In fact, studies have shown that 70 percent of all college students who don't complete college fail to do so because they have poor time-management and study skills. Since few schools overtly teach such skills, one of your tasks as parents is to ensure that your child is well equipped in these areas.

One of your key roles is to ensure that your child understands the importance of handing in all assignments, on time. This is crucial not only because doing homework significantly improves test performance, but also because even a few zeros on homework assignments will have a devastating effect on a student's overall average.

Let's take an example: Suppose a class has four graded homework assignments. Student #1 hands them all in on time and gets an 80 on each. Average grade: 80 (obviously).

Student #2 hands in three assignments — again getting 80's on all three — but doesn't hand in the fourth. Average grade for Student #2 is 60. One missed assignment out of four cuts the average grade by 20 points!

Similarly, handing in assignments late usually hurts a student's grade since teachers usually only give partial credit for late work. While you can't absolutely ensure your child turns in every assignment on time, you CAN take steps to ensure that your child's teachers let you know immediately if your child fails to hand in any assignments. I'll show you how to set up this valuable response in the Administrative Support Section.

Summary

You, the parent, will support the academic system by providing time, space, and encouragement for your child to complete class assignments. This is not the time to question the value or logic of assignments nor the teacher's motives. This is the time to teach your child that work on any assigned taks, whether for grades in school or salary on the job, will have a completion requirement. The teacher cannot give your child 60 minutes of a class period to explain or answer all of his or her questions. Realistically, the concept introduced in class can be learned better by review and repetition of work assignments. This takes time out of class that is in and under your control. You must be responsible for teaching your child how to use time management skills outside of the classroom.

TEACHING YOUR CHILD
TIME-MANAGEMENT SKILLS

Time-management skills help develop behavior patterns that are conducive to making good grades. The best way to send the message to your child that education comes first is to develop a time-management calendar around school work. This does not mean a child can't go to soccer practice after school or participate in other extracurricular activities — as long as grades are at an acceptable level. If not, the schedule should be adjusted in order to spend more time on the subject or subjects in which performance is unsatisfactory.

Children aren't born with a well-developed sense of priorities, so one of your responsibilities as a parent is to help develop such a sense. This will sometimes mean that soccer practice will have to wait until the grades improve. And no, this won't win you any popularity contests.

Of course, you might also have to adjust your schedule in order to enforce the time-management schedule you and your child have agreed upon, but hopefully this will only be a temporary disruption.

The following page is an example of a time-management schedule. The schedule should be as specific and detailed as possible. The student should spend at least SOME time studying each subject each day. This doesn't mean your child must spend an hour studying math, an hour studying English, and an hour studying science every day, but that he or she must at least REVIEW each subject every day. (We'll discuss the most efficient ways to review later in this book.)

Figure #1:
Example of an afterschool
time-management schedule.

AFTER-CLASS STUDY SCHEDULE

Name ———————————————————— Date ——————

	MONDAY	TUESDAY	WEDNESDAY	THURSDAY	FRIDAY
3:00					
3:30					
4:00					
4:30					
5:00					
5:30					
6:00					
6:30					
7:00					
7:30					
8:00					
8:30					
9:00					
9:30					
10:00					

Parent's
Initials ———   ———   ———   ———   ———

Monday: In addition to a student's regular homework, the student should study vocabulary or spelling words. After studying the words, the parent should test the child.

Tuesday: In addition to the regular homework, the student should study the words he missed on Monday. The parent should then test the child over the words he missed on Monday. There is no need to spend time studying all the words.

Wednesday: Repeat the process.

Thursday: Study all the words. Parents should test the student over all words. Student should intensively study the words he missed.

Friday: Student should score high on the test!

Often, vocabulary and spelling tests count the same as chapter tests. It is important for students to score high on tests where they know the questions, like vocabulary or spelling tests. (See Figure #2.) This will help to offset possible low scores on subjective or more difficult tests.

Anytime a student is tested over lists (for example states and capitals), the list should be broken down into smaller lists. The smaller lists should be studied and mastered every night. Studying for a test a little each night eliminates having to "cram" the night before the test.

Even if a teacher says "No homework tonight," your child MUST still review his or her notes for that class. It's best to study the hardest subjects first. Students should study at the same time and place every day, in a place free from distractions. This means NO TELEPHONE, TELEVISION, RADIOS, or similar distractions.

In English and foreign language courses, students are usually given a list of vocabulary words that they will be tested over each week. Students should study this list each night. Students often have spelling and vocabulary words to learn every week.

Summary

Home schedules will go through a transition period as time-management skills are taught. This is a good example of what happens in the average classroom when a new concept is introduced. The family will not find a structured time schedule at home an easy task; it will take some work on organizational skills for everyone because everyone is involved. At first, you, as parens, have to be involved in seeing that the review and study time does take place. This means everyone in the family will feel the affects of a new schedule and will be prepared for some rough times.

TEACHING YOUR CHILD
ORGANIZATIONAL SKILLS

Organizational skills are a major problem for most students, especially when they move from elementary school to middle school or junior high school. Surprisingly, a simple three-ring binder or notebook can be a powerful tool to help your child become better organized. At the same time, it will also help you monitor your child's progress in each class.

The notebook should be a sturdy, one- or two-inch, three-ring binder with pockets in the front and back and dividers for each subject. (It may be necessary to purchase the dividers separately.) The notebook should go with your child to every class and home with the child every night. If you pick up your child from school, make sure he has his notebook. If he doesn't, he should go back and get it.

Using the Notebook

Behind each divider should be a daily class schedule sheet. (See Figure #2 for an example you can copy). The purpose of this sheet is to help keep track of class assignments. Each day, for each class, the student should write down what is done in that class. Every class should have an entry each day, even if the teacher does not give an assignment. This helps both parents and the student keep track of what the student is doing in each subject.

The class schedule has a place for the date, the assignment the day it is due, and the grade the student received on that assignment. Above the grade column is a grade goal line. The student should put what he wants to make at the end of a grading period on this line. At the end of each week, the parent and student should average the grades. If your child is not reaching his or her grade goal, you should jointly develop a plan on what the child can do differently the next week in order to bring up his grade.

The pockets in the front and back of the notebook will help students keep track of their homework assignments. All homework assignments go in the front cover of the notebook — not in the front pocket of the jeans, not the front pocket of the coat, not in the front cover of the textbook. All completed homework assignments go in the front pocket of the notebook. When the teacher says, "Get out your homework," the student will know exactly where to look.

When the student has completed his homework for the evening, the notebook and the school books should be stacked by the door. Before the child goes to bed, you should check to make sure the homework is in the front pocket of the notebook and that all books are by the door, ready for school the next day. Students should get in the habit of putting the

THE WAY TO AN "A"

Figure #2

Course _____

Grade Goal _____

Date	Date Due	Assignment	Grade	Parent or Teacher Signature

books in the same place every night. This will reduce the chances of forgetting them when the student leaves for school the next morning.

The notebook will also be the filing place for book surveys and chapter surveys. These are discussed in detail elsewhere in this book.

Summary

The notebook is a powerful tool which can help your child become more organized — and hopefully will introduce him or her to the benefits of good organization. It should go with the student to every class and home with the student every night. The notebook also provides a way for parents to check on their child's assignments and progress. When your child comes home from school, don't ask, "What did you do in school today?" Say, "Let me check your notebook."

HELPING YOUR CHILD
SCORE HIGH ON TESTS
AND ASSIGNMENTS

In the section entitled "What Students Can Do," I describe several techniques or methods which will help improve academic performance. These techniques will teach your child how to study a book, how to take notes from a textbook, how to take notes from lectures, and how to review these notes in order to score high on tests.

Your job as parents (i.e., management!) is to ensure that your child actually APPLIES these techniques to his or her school work each day. To do this, you'll need to read the Student section to learn what's involved in using these tools and what to expect from your child by using this approach. For the moment,

I've briefly summarized each technique below.

The first technique is the *book survey*. It helps students to understand what the textbook is about before they start studying the individual chapters.

The *chapter survey* does for each chapter what the book survey does for the entire book. It teaches your child how to extract the most important information from each chapter in an efficient way.

Students have a responsibility to apply the techniques of surveying texts, reading, and review. However, they must also learn to take notes.

Note-taking from lecture is a listening skill that most students have not developed. Think about the number of times you have to repeat what you have asked your child to do and transfer this to the classroom setting. The students must learn to listen and take notes in order to recognize the important information rather than trying to record every word.

My method of review has proved to be successful for most students. Your child will learn a new pattern which teaches retention rather than one which encourages a quick memorization for a next-day test.

SETTING GOALS

Setting goals is an important part of being successful, both in school and after graduation. Parents can teach their child short-term goal-setting by using grades. Parents should also discuss midrange and long-range goals with their child. An example of a long-range goal would be to explore what the child would like to be when he or she grows up. Midrange goals are goals that must be accomplished in order for a person to achieve their long-range goals. For example, a college education is essential if a person wants to enter a number of professions.

A study was done of the 1953 graduating class

of Yale University. The study asked how many members of the graduating class had written long-term goals. Three percent had. Twenty years later, they did a follow-up study and found that the three percent who had written long-term goals were worth more financially than the other 97 percent combined.

The above example shows how important and powerful goal setting can be. Start teaching your child how to set and reach goals at an early age by using grades. To help you do this, the "class schedule" (see Figure #2) has a place for grade goals in each subject.

If you are not reaching your grade goal, have you:

1. Deviated from your time management schedule?
2. Recorded all class assignments and kept your grade average?
3. Turned in all assignments on time?
4. Completed your chapter survey before the teacher introduced it?
5. Reviewed your notes every night and changed the order of review?
6. Attended all classes and arrived on time?
7. Followed the test-taking tips?
8. Asked the teacher for extra help?
9. Gotten your teacher on your team by not being a discipline problem?
10. Maintained a positive attitude?

Summary

Since goals are necessary for success in any activity from games to careers, write down and discuss short-term, midrange, and long-range goals. These may change, but at the present write down what the goals seem to be. This would be a positive activity for all family members.

THE PARENTS' ROLE IN HOMEWORK

Each day, when the child comes home from school, the parent should check his or her notebook. This should be done consistently each day and preferably as soon as the child gets home from school.

The parent should first check the daily class schedule sheet. There should be an entry each day for each subject. If the child gets a graded paper back, the grade should be recorded. At the end of each week, the grades should be averaged in each class. The average should be compared to the grade goal. If the child is not reaching his goal, devise a plan to determine what can be done differently next week in order to bring up the grade average.

Check all papers that have been graded and returned to the student. Go over problems that the student has missed.

It is not necessary for a parent to sit by his child's side while he is doing his homework. In fact, it is not recommended. A parent should provide a quiet place for the child to study. It should be in the same place everyday. It should be away from distractions. No telephone. No stereo. No television. No radio. No headphones.

The child should do as much of the homework as possible before asking the parent for help. The parent's primary goal is to help the child become an independent learner. After the child has completed as much homework as possible independently, the child may ask the parent for help. As the school year progresses, try to spend less and less time helping your child with homework.

As your child grows older, you will probably spend less time helping him or her with homework and more time monitoring and enforcing the study schedule.

After the student has completed his homework, check all assignments to make sure they are correct. The questions or problems that were missed should be corrected by the child.

Your main role in your child's homework is to enforce the study schedule. Remember, an essential factor in raising your child's grades is the consistency with which this plan is enforced.

An important tool to help you monitor your child's progress in each course is the class format sheet (See Figure #3). This gives you a good idea of what's going on in each class without having to depend entirely on what your child tells you. With a completed class format sheet, you can help your child avoid the classic night-before-it's-due, 2000-word term paper panic. Similarly, if you know from the class format sheet that your child's English teacher always gives a spelling test on Fridays, your child is less likely to get away with "I don't have any homework" on Thursday night.

You can put this tool to work by simply asking the teacher if she would please fill out the enclosed class format sheet and return it to you in a week (give date) in the self-addressed, stamped envelope you've enclosed.

Summary

Homework is for the student; seeing that homework is done becomes the parents' responsibility. To make your job easier, incorporate what you are teaching your child: get the administration on your team by getting a class format sheet, provide the environment for the homework, and schedule a homework check time. Most of all, do what you say you will do.

Figure #3: Example of class format sheet.

CLASS FORMAT SHEET

Student's Name: —————————— Date: —————

Teacher's Name: ————————————————————

Subject: ——————— Planning Period: —————

What chapters or material will you cover during this grading period?

Is extra credit available?
If so, please specify.

Do you schedule a specific assignment or test on a weekly basis? (Example: spelling test or vocabulary test.)

Will you assign a major report or test during this grading period? Please specify.

THE PARENTS' ROLE IN
ADMINISTRATIVE SUPPORT

Just as you have far better time-management skills than your child (you DO, don't you?), you are a great deal better equipped to deal effectively with other adults than your child is. So one of the things you can do to help your child is what might be called "administrative support." This can be viewed as getting the adult-run "system" to work WITH or FOR you and your child.

We've all been through years of indoctrination with the school system. Parents are often told that they are "only the parent" and that they should leave the business of educating their child to the "experts."

You MUST banish the "I am only the parent" mentality and replace it with "I am the boss. I am the taxpayer. I pay the bills. You work for me." You must constantly keep in mind that you are the real power, that you have the authority to make changes, that you have the right to require quality education for your child, that you have the parental obligation to demand RESULTS.

This chapter will help you meet these challenges.

Parent-Teacher Contact

Effective communication with teachers and the principal will improve school life for your child. Volunteer in the school when possible. Attend PTA meetings and conferences. Be visible. Be vocal. Your communication with the school system, visibility, interest, and willingness to put forth unusual effort will ensure that your child gets his or her fair share of the teacher's time and attention and will enhance his overall school experience.

Communications with your child's teachers can

be divided into two broad categories: (1) those that you can initiate to avoid problems and (2) communications that take place should a problem arise.

Start the school year off the right way by writing a letter to each of your child's teachers. Tell each teacher that you want to be actively involved in your child's education, that you want to be a working partner with the teacher and the school.

Let the teacher know that education is a priority in your home. Tell him/her that although you encourage your child to participate in afterschool activities, school work comes first. Inform the teacher that you require your child to study each subject every day and that a vital part of your monitoring program is the class format sheet which you've enclosed.

Inform the teacher that you require your child to do all homework assignments and turn them in whether your child gets credit for doing them or not. Ask her to inform you of missing assignments by returning the self-addressed postcard. When you get a postcard in the mail, have your child do the missing assignment immediately and return it to the teacher by mail or hand deliver it to her.

It is important that the assignment be made up and returned to the teacher as soon as possible. Do not send it back to the school with your child since the chances of it getting lost may be substantial.

MISSING ASSIGNMENT POSTCARD

```
                                    ┌──────────┐
                                    │  Stamp   │
                                    │          │
                                    └──────────┘

        _____
              Self-Adddfressed
        _____

                          _____
```

You may use this format in making your postcard.
Keep it simple so a busy teacher can get it in the mail.

```
Student's name _____  Date _____

Missing Assignment _____

Behavior

    ☐ Good              ☐ Talks too much

Remarks

                                    GPA _____
```

Inform the teacher that your child is required to keep his own grades, but every two weeks would he/she check to see that the self-reported grades are the same as those in the grade book.

After you have completed the letter, write "copy to:" at the bottom of the page, followed by the principal's name. Then MAIL A COPY TO THE PRINCIPAL. This does two things: It lets the principal know what you've asked the teacher to do; and perhaps more importantly, it lets the teacher know that you are in touch with the principal.

Now write a SEPARATE letter to the principal. Tell the principal that you look forward to working with him or her this year, and that if there is a problem with your child, you would like to be informed immediately. Include your telephone number at work as well as at home.

The letters to the teacher and principal should be positive and firm. You want to let both parties know that you support the school system, but you would "highly appreciate it" if your child's teachers would fill out and return the class format sheets. Also if your child misses an assignment, you would appreciate it if the teacher would return the postcards you have sent them. Finally, you'd appreciate the teacher's cooperation in doing the two-week grade check.

Examples of the letters to teachers and the principal are shown on the following pages. Note that the letter is written from a masculine point of view. The mother can write the letter, the mother can type the letter, but if possible, both parents should sign it. Unfair as it might seem, the bottom line is that fathers still seem to have more clout.

On occasion, a teacher won't return the class format sheet in a timely manner. In that case, you should call and ask the teacher to return it. If it does not arrive within the week, then contact the principal. If this doesn't produce results, contact the school superintendent. In the unlikely event that you still don't get the cooperation you seek, contact the school board.

Teachers and principals must be held accountable. A lot is being said about school reform these days, but the best way to improve the school that your child attends is to get actively involved in your child's education and to make the schools accountable. After all, you're paying their salaries, you're the taxpayer.

New class format letters should be sent out at the beginning of each grading period. The best time to do this is when the child gets his report card.

Very few adults will be surprised to hear that teachers love to get letters of appreciation. Writing such letters to your child's teachers offers an easy way to keep in contact with the teacher. As an aside, writing letters of appreciation when the teacher does something special for your child makes the teacher look good with the school administration — a point that won't go unnoticed by the teacher. Be sure to send a copy of the letter to the principal.

Sample Letters

1. Sample of "pre-emptive" letter to teachers:

Dear [Teacher's name]:

Education has a very high priority in our family. My wife and I intend to be active participants in our child's education. We believe working together with our child's teachers as a team is the best way to ensure our child's academic success.

[Child's name] is on a structured study program

which requires [him/her] to study each subject each night. In order for us to better assist [him/her] in a more effective way at home, would you please fill out the enclosed class format sheet and return it by [one week from date of letter]? I've enclosed an addressed, stamped envelope for your convenience. Thank you very much.

It's our understanding that not turning in assignments is one of the major causes of low grades. Accordingly, it is vital that we know as soon as possible if [child's name] should fail to submit any assignments, so we can take proper action.

If [child's name] misses an assignment, would you please fill out the enclosed self-addressed postcard and mail it to me immediately? I will see that [Name] does the work and turns it in, even if no credit will be earned.

[Child's name] is required to keep track of [his/her] own grades, but every two weeks we would appreciate a grade check from you to ensure our information is accurate.

Of course, if there are any problems concerning [child's name]'s behavior or attitude, we would like to be the first to know. Please call us at [phone number].

Again, we strongly believe that your cooperation is vital if this plan is to succeed. If you have any suggestions on how we can improve our plan or ways in which we can assist our child to succeed in your class, we would welcome such input. Otherwise, we will look forward to receiving the class format sheet by [date] and postcards if [child's name] misses an assignment.

Sincerely,

Mr. & Mrs. Parent

cc: [Principal's name]

2. Sample Letter to Principal:

Dear [Principal's name]:

My wife and I look forward to working with the school this year to ensure that our child gets a quality education. We have been very pleased with the emphasis that [name of school] places on academics and on the high standards it sets for students.

I have enclosed a copy of a letter we have sent to all of [child's name]'s teachers. I would greatly appreciate it if you would follow up on this and reinforce the importance of returning the class format sheets and postcards promptly.

Thank you for your cooperation in this matter. I would also like to take this opportunity to thank you and your staff for all the hard work and unusual effort that has gone into making [name of school] an institution where education comes first and students are the main priority.

Sincerely,

Mr. & Mrs. Parent

P.S. If there is a discipline problem with [child's name], I would like to be the first to know. Please call me at [home number] or [work number].

3. "The Ultimate Weapon"
Sample Letter to School Board Members:

Dear _____:

I am sure you understand how vitally important it is for parents to take an active role in their child's education. As parents, my wife and I have a strong commitment to education and feel that one of our most important responsibilities as parents is to see that our child receives a quality education. Obviously, we need the help and cooperation of the school system to fulfill this responsibility, and it is my understanding that the policy of this school system is to encourage parental involvement.

At the beginning of the school year, I wrote the enclosed letter to all of my child's teachers. I also wrote a letter to the principal and have enclosed a copy for your reference.

One week later, I had not received letters from [number] of my child's teachers. I then called each one on the phone requesting that they return the class format sheet and return postcard in the event my [child] missed an assignment.

Last week, after my call, I had [number] teacher(s) return the sheet. I then called the principal requesting help. It is now almost midway into the grading period, and I still have not had full cooperation from the school. [Number] teacher(s) [has/have] still not returned my letter.

I believe part of the reason my child is not doing as well as we would like in [name of subject(s)] is the teacher's lack of cooperation. I believe that it is your responsibility as an elected school board member to ensure that teachers and administrators cooperate with parents in trying to get the best possible performance from students. I believe that it is my responsibility, as a parent and taxpayer, to bring this to your attention.

Thank you for your immediate attention to this problem. Please contact me as soon as possible regarding the outcome of this correspondence.

Sincerely,
Mr. & Mrs. Parent

Figure #4:
Schedule for sending "pre-emptive letters

This schedule can be adjusted if your child's school does not follow the nine-week grading period. It can also be adjusted when your child has reached the desired grade goals.

Week #1
Write letters to the principal and teachers, following the sample letters in this book.

Week #2
Ask your child for a grade check. (See page 43 for sample grade check sheet.)
If your child has not completed the grade check by Wednesday afternoon, call the school Thursday morning and request they do one.
If your child did the grade check on his/her own and had each teacher's signature (not the teacher's name signed by a friend), he/she should be praised and even rewarded for putting forth unusual effort and for showing responsibility and maturity. If he/she has no zeros, the praise should be even greater. If he/she has zeros, make sure he/she makes them up immediately, If you did not receive a postcard from the teacher informing you of the missing assignment, call the teacher and request postcards for missing assignments in the future.
If class format sheets aren't returned, call the teachers and ask them to return them. Also, remind them to return postcards if your child misses an assignment.

Week #3
If class format sheets are not returned, call principal.

Send letters of appreciation to teachers if appropriate.

Send a copy of the letters to the principal.

Week #4

Call for grade checks. Follow the same procedure as Week #2. If you have not received class format sheets and postcards, call the school superintendent.

Week #5

If you still have not received information from the teachers, write school board members. An example of such a letter is shown on page 39.

Week #6

Do a grade check. Follow the same procedure as in Week #2.

Week #7

Write letters of appreciation. Send a copy of each of these letters to the principal.

Week #8

Do a grade check.

If you still have not received the full cooperation from the teachers and you have called the principal and followed up with letters to the school board members, now it's time to write a letter to the editor of your local newspaper. Use the same style as the letter to school board members.

Week #9

Take the week off (as far as your child's school work, anyway).

Week #10

Write thank you letters and send new class format sheets.

GRADE CHECK

Name _____ Date _____

According to my records, my current grade average is as follows. If your records agree with mine, please sign under teacher's signature.

	SUBJECT	MISSING ASSIGNMENTS	GRADE AVERAGE	TEACHER'S SIGNATURE
1				
2				
3				
4				
5				
6				

By following this plan, you have the opportunity of modifying the behavior patterns of your child, teachers, administrators, and school board members. This is no small accomplishment! In most cases, this plan will have accomplished the desired goal of providing the necessary tools for your child's education. However, if you still need help, your next action will be to enlist the help of the parent organization in your district and/or write a letter to the editor of your newspaper.

Summary

Communication is a basic requirement when there is a team working toward a common goal. Every member is vital to the success of your child's education. You, the parent have the most power to see that there is no breakdown in the communication. Use your position to ensure the success your child deserves. If all members are meeting their individual responsibilities, but your child is not able to meet the short-term academic goals, call for a conference.

HOW TO HAVE EFFECTIVE PARENT-TEACHER CONFERENCES

One of the main reasons for writing those "preemptive letters" was to reduce the likelihood of any trouble. Unfortunately, even the best precautions don't always have the desired effect, so what do you do if the school tags your delightful child as a troublemaker or something similar? The most important thing is to put every communication in writing.

Communicating with the school in writing is very important because it documents everything in case things are not resolved to your satisfaction. You should keep a copy of everything you send to the school. Conversations with teachers are fine, but you should follow up with a letter.

Parent-teacher conferences are usually dreaded by both parents and teachers. On the parents' part, this dread probably stems from the fact that such conferences are usually held because there is a problem with their child. Thus parents often feel on the defensive from the outset. (And of course, some parents BECOME highly defensive on hearing their child criticized by other adults.) It is normal to be nervous about a meeting where there is going to be an unpleasant problem discussed. It may help you to know that most educators do not have educational courses which prepare them for these conferences.

Consider the teacher's viewpoint: The conference is usually held at the end of a long working day. Many teachers have experienced not only verbal but physical attacks at conferences; and they, like you, would rather not have conflicts. Emotional parents often claim the problem is the teacher's fault and may question the teacher's ability to teach, the method of controlling the classroom, or how discipline problems are handled. In any case, the teacher is expected to solve the problem because the educator is "the expert." This frequently — and understandably — causes the teacher to become defensive.

Thus, the first objective in a parent-teacher conference is for the parent not to become or feel defensive, nor should the parent make the teacher feel defensive. Attitude will be a key factor to the success of this conference.

What do you want from this conference? Consider all possible solutions — both positive and negative. What can you accept? As you set your mind to this goal, realize you may encounter the same strong will of an educator. Be honest with yourself and your expectations.

The purpose of a parent-teacher conference is to address any problems your child has and to discuss ways to solve them. In order to have a successful conference, it is important to identify the factors you would like to address at the meeting and what you would like to have accomplished. This is called an agenda, and it should include a brief description of the problem as you see it and suggestions for solving it. Be sure you state the problem as one which the child has rather than one which the teacher has. An example of an agenda is shown on the next page (Figure 5).

Plan what to wear to the conference. If you want to be taken seriously, then present yourself in a serious manner. What you wear can say a lot about you, so your dress should be neat, clean, and conservative.

Plan who should go to the meeting with you. If at all possible, both parents should attend the conference. If this is impossible, take a relative or a friend. What you're looking for is someone who can give you emotional support and independently verify your recollections and impressions if needed.

The conference time is usually limited, so make sure every minute is productive. The problem should be identified in the first few minutes. Think of the identification period as only a fourth to a third of the total conference time. More than half of the conference should be spent on how to solve the problem. Prepare a folder of your child's class work. The papers, test scores, and/or report cards may help identify the seed of the problem which exists at this time. Good papers would also be a way to show the teachers the potential you know your child has. Poor grades or papers are not a reflection of your parenting skills. The system moved your child to this grade

Figure #5

AGENDA FOR
PARENT/TEACHER CONFERENCE
regarding
(name of student)

(date)

Problem: [Summarize the problem as you see it. Be sure to phrase this summary as a problem the child has rather than a problem the school has. Example:]

(Name of student) is not meeting his projected grade goal. The hard work and extra effort (child's name) is putting forth does not seem to be reflected in the grade point average. This is causing frustration and low self-esteem and may result in future discipline problems.

Attempts to solve the problem by parents include:
1. Letters to teachers requesting course information.
2. Post cards to be returned if (name) misses an assignment.
3. (Name) is required to keep his own grades but periodic grade checks have been requested by parents.
4. (Name) is required to study (specified subject) each night.

Suggestions from teachers and administrators:

level. Now, they have the obligation to make recommendations for a follow-up to see that your child achieves the academic goals of this level.

It is a good idea to take a tape recorder to the meeting. Make sure the recorder has batteries and is in working order. Have a notepad and pen (that works) to make notes of questions which may come to your mind while someone is speaking.

At the conference:

Arrive early for the meeting. When the teacher (or teachers) enters the room, you should initiate the conversation, since this conveys an impression of self-confidence and control. Begin by introducing yourself to the teacher.

After you are seated, get out the tape recorder and place it on the table. There is no need to ask permission to use it. Next, send around a sign-in sheet, which should include the name, position, and best time to be reached for everyone present.

After the sign-up sheet has gone around the room, hand out your agenda and read it aloud.

Be prepared to hear things about your child that may be negative or undesirable. Comments may be made about you that are negative or undesirable. This is a good time to take notes to keep from interrupting or becoming argumentative. Take a few seconds to consider what was said. It does not hurt to say you may be asked to respond to those comments later. Your main objective must not be lost at this time. By showing respect after hearing a verbal criticism, you may establish more control of the conference.

Don't let negative comments from teachers or principals make you defensive. Often negative comments can be turned around and used to your advantage.

For example, if a school administrator states that your child is doing poorly in school and is a discipline problem, simply state that the administrator is right. You know your child is *having problems* in school, that is why you are here, and you hope this meeting will offer solutions to correct the problem.

Do not speak negatively of your child. When possible, say positive things about your child. If the teacher says your child has the potential to do better, but is just lazy; then capitalize on the child's potential. You might respond by saying, "Yes, I know my child has the potential. Previous tests and grades have provided that opinion." Impress the school that as a team of adults there has to be a solution to the question of how to educate this child. You have come to the professional educators for positive recommendations.

Help the school personnel develop a positive attitude toward your child. You must convince the staff that, with the right guidance, your child is bright and capable of overcoming any problems.

If a teacher or administrator continues to make derogatory comments about your child, write down everything that is said, trying to get every word. Again, this keeps you calm and busy, but it is crucial to your next power play. When the insult is completed, say in your polite, positive tone, "Do you have anything else to add?" Either continue to take notes, or if there is no additional comment, state that you want to read your notes to confirm what you have heard. In a calm voice, slowly read every word, and then ask if the notes are correct. Make any corrections and ask for verification. The words may change with each reading; however, you are the one in control. If necessary, rewind the tape. Do whatever is necessary to make sure you have correctly identified all possible factors in this problem.

It is important to drop the matter and continue the meeting in a businesslike manner as quickly as possible. Handling such situations in this manner shows school personnel that you are in control and implies that you will report future derogatory comments to the proper authorities.

Don't allow school officials to put you on the defensive. Never apologize for someone else's mistakes. Don't allow school personnel to intimidate you. If you don't understand what a term means, ask that it be explained. If a school employee states that there is a certain policy, rule etc. that requires them to take action or not to take action, ask to see the policy and obtain an official copy.

Always stay calm. The calmer you are, the better the impression you make as an informed parent who is confident and in control. If the school official loses his/her control, you have just gained points for your side. Past experience indicates that the one who keeps calm is the one who is in control.

Everyone came to the conference because he or she contributes to the child's development; therefore, allow everyone to speak. Practice your listening skills; be polite even when you want to interrupt. When you feel the need to interrupt, take notes. It would be to your advantage to be able to note something positive the educator says and repeat it as well as anything negative you want to correct.

Some schools have a procedure which dictates whether the student is a part of the conference; however, when the decision is left up to you, use the opportunity to have your child witness the number of people concerned about this problem. The student should hear the problem defined and speak with respect when questioned. The student should be present when the teacher proposes solutions to the problem and should be given the opportunity to offer his or her own solutions. The student should listen respectfully and not speak unless asked a question. At the end of the meeting, the student should be given an opportunity to comment or voice his or her opinion.

Your child should be excused from the conference when you are discussing areas on which you and the teachers or administrators don't agree. The parents and teachers should appear, in the child's eyes, as a united team helping to ensure that he or she gets the best education possible. Parents should not speak of the teachers or administrators in a negative manner. When parents show respect for teachers, this teaches children to show respect also.

After the conference:

Write the school personnel a letter thanking them for meeting with you. In the letter, summarize the meeting and restate the problems and possible solutions. The follow-up letter is very important, primarily because it documents the conference. The letter should also encourage school personnel to take immediate action to solve the problem. After all, the success of the conference depends on the action taken after the conference.

Talk to your child about the conference. Discuss the problem and the suggested solutions. Ask if your child has any thoughts about the conference. Were all problems and solutions discussed thoroughly? Ask for any suggestions on how you can improve future conferences. Praise the child's good conduct and behavior during the meeting.

If you feel the outcome of the conference was unsatisfactory, you should feel free to discuss your concerns with someone higher in the administration. By doing so, you are telling school officials that you do not agree with a school policy or recommendation which affects your child, and you are requesting that they review and reconsider the decision.

Parents should appeal if they feel their child's educational needs are not being met. An example would be if your child is put in a group where his abilities are not being challenged or he is not receiving adequate remedial help. Parents should also appeal if a child receives punishment for an act he did not commit or is subjected to verbal or physical abuse. Parents should also consider appealing if their child's grade is reduced because of tardiness, absences, or other behavior not directly related to academic performance.

When you decide to appeal, it is important to follow the proper procedures. First, request a copy of the policies related to the issue you are appealing. Make sure school personnel are following school policies and procedures.

When appealing, always put your requests in writing. State the problem and why the situation is not good for your child. Explain how you would like to see the problem solved and include a date by which you would like to have a reply or action. Ask school officials to commit to a timetable for results. This should be mailed to the superintendent. A follow-up may be necessary; this starts with an appointment with the superintendent.

Follow up on all meetings and phone calls with a letter restating what was discussed and agreed on at the meeting. This follow-up letter is very important, so be sure to not overlook this vital step. If you are still dissatisfied, talk to the school board members.

School boards are usually eager and willing to talk to parents; however, you can appreciate the fact school boards are not elected to know the day-to-day routine of every classroom. As a result, school board members typically turn to the administration for answers. The larger the school district, the more removed the board members' relationship will be to you. They are burdened with the legal and financial problems of the district, and too often they depend on the staff to establish policies and relate to the public for them.

If you still have not received satisfaction after talking to the school board members, contact state officials and/or write a letter to the editor of the local newspaper.

One of the best ways to win an appeal, to effect change in policy, and to make your child's school a more effective learning institution is for parents to organize. There is power in numbers, but you do not need large numbers in the beginning. You can start with a small group of committed parents.

These parents may be facing the same problems and frustrations you are. Decide the purpose of your group. Set short- and long-term goals. Make your goals specific and measurable. You should also set a timetable in which to achieve your goals.

You obviously do not need permission or approval from school officials to organize a parent group. On the other hand, it would be courteous to inform them of your plans.

Summary

The term "conference" registers negative associations for many parents and educators, but a positive attitude does much to help you look at this meeting as a positive step toward academic recovery for your child. Plan ahead, know why you are having a conference, do any research that is necessary, take equipment and proof of your position, and think of this as the meeting of those who can and will provide what your child needs for a foundation for life.

CHOOSING YOUR CHILD'S TEACHERS:
The key to a successful year

Teachers are probably the number one factor that determines if your child has a successful school year. Parents have a right to choose which teacher their child has; after all, they are paying for it.

When choosing a teacher, try not to judge solely on a teacher's reputation. A teacher that is right for one child may not be right for another. Observe in the prospective teacher's class and decide for yourself.

The best time to observe your child's future teachers is the first two hours in the morning. Some schools have parent visitation day. However, visiting at this time may not be a true representation of the typical day. A better idea may be to call the school a few weeks before school is out and ask to observe in specific classes. Inform the principal that you would like to observe teachers that your child may have next year. Tell the principal that you want to make sure your child's teacher next year has a teaching style that is compatible to your child's learning style.

In the classroom, look for a child who is similar to yours in learning ability and in behavior. Identifying a child who is similar to yours is important. Most teachers work fine with bright students who are well behaved, but it is much more of a challenge to work with students who are slow learners or overactive.

Choosing teachers at the secondary level is also important. By the time your child is a teenager, he is usually an excellent judge of good teachers. Counselors, school secretaries, and other teachers can also give you suggestions on teachers who would be appropriate for your child.

Inform college students that it is often as important to choose a professor as it is to choose a course. Colleges and universities often have master teachers they use as a drawing card to attract students and give their school credibility in the eyes of the business community and alumni. Students should enroll in these professors' courses. Even if their major is not in a certain professor's field, the students can often take a course under this professor as an elective.

The best time to request a teacher is a week or two before school ends. Make an appointment with the principal. At the meeting, be positive about the school and your child. Communicate to the principal that your child's education is a top priority and that by working together with the school, as a team, is the best way to ensure that your child gets a good education.

Describe your child to the principal in a positive light and ask which teacher he would recommend for your child. He will probably not tell you, but it never hurts to ask, and you are planting a seed without actually coming right out and requesting a teacher. Inform the principal that you will occasionally visit your child's classroom and that you will help the teachers and volunteer in the school as much as possible. In requesting a certain teacher, never say that one teacher seems better than another, but rather mention the personalities would seem to be a better combination. Your child has probably not been assigned to a class yet, and by letting the principal know that you will be actively involved and present in the classroom, you will enhance the chances of your child being assigned to the best teacher or teachers.

What if you did not get the teacher who is appropriate for your child and you need to change teachers? A week or two before school starts, go to the school to confirm the classroom selection. Ask for an immediate conference to ascertain why the request was not granted. The principal's answer determines your next course of action. Either accept the decision or repeat the process of calling on the superintendent and going as far in the steps as you feel are necessary.

There are times when a child needs to be moved into a different classroom after the school year has begun. This is difficult on all concerned. Educators know it can have an effect similar to a land run. The class size will be changed. How will this reflect on your child? The move will make additional work for the new teacher. Remember, everyone has an emotion that will be triggered by this request. If at all possible, seek a transfer from the class rather than the teacher. Administrators must be made aware of ineffective teachers, but the immediate concern is getting your child into an appropriate educational environment. Use all of the polite methods to move the child, consider the consequences of exposing the reasons for moving your child, and prepare the administrator for your steps to evaluate and confirm with documentation the need for a change.

Things to look for when observing in the classroom:

1. Is the classroom environment warm and friendly? Is the room interesting? Are the exhibits and bulletin boards designed to be attractive, yet educational? Teachers who spend extra time and effort to make their learning environment stimula-ting and interesting usually go the extra mile to make sure their curriculum is also stimulating and interesting, a place where students enjoy learning.

2. Are most students "on task" most of the time? Are they spending most of their time on relevant academic activities? Studies have shown that the average percentage of class time spent on

learning tasks is as high as 85 percent with some teachers and as low as 20 percent with others.

3. Does the teacher maintain good and consistent discipline? Many teachers can change a student's behavior simply by giving the student a certain look; others find it necessary to verbally embarrass a student by constant reprimands.

4. Does the teacher use time wisely? Does the teacher spend a minimal amount of time on housekeeping activities like calling roll and handing back papers? Does class start as soon as the bell rings?

5. Does the teacher teach the students or the subject? Does the teacher appear to have a genuine concern for the students? Most teachers know the power and influence they have over their students. They believe that they can make a difference. One good teacher can make the difference in whether a child continues in school or becomes a dropout. In retrospect, a teacher's scorn can also cause a student's self-esteem and attitude to nose-dive. Some teachers teach subjects such as English and math; good teachers teach students.

6. Does the teacher meet the needs of individual students or are all students taught the same way? Does the teacher show as well as tell in order to meet the needs of the visual as well as the auditory learner? Does the teacher vary the difficulty of each assignment to meet the needs of the gifted students as well as those of the less able learner?

7. Is the teacher well educated and qualified to teach the subject? If the teacher loves the subject being taught, that love and enthusiasm for the subject is often passed on to the students.

8. Do students think this teacher is a good teacher? We often overlook the best person to judge teacher performance and that is the student. Ask students who have had the teacher in the past if they would like to have the teacher again. If the answer is yes, the chances are this person is a good teacher.

9. Does the teacher praise positive behavior and reward work well done? When possible, the teacher should ignore negative behavior and praise positive behavior. When teachers are positive and lavish with their praise toward their students, students are much more willing to respond to their direction and assistance.

10. Does the teacher encourage the students to want more information on the topic being studied and allow related questions? Does the teacher respect each question? This encourages self-disciplined behavior and confidence in the child.

These observations will help you be a better judge in selecting the best teacher for your child. The teacher has a direct relationship to the success for the school year for your child.

Summary

Since teachers play such an important role in the success or failure of a school year for your child, you will assure your child's success by working with the teachers and administration very closely. You will be a positive, visible parent doing what is necessary to help provide the academic environment your child requires. Involved parents are able to find ways to be at school during the school day or at evening activities. No matter when or what you are doing at school, you will listen, observe, and make new friends which will benefit your child.

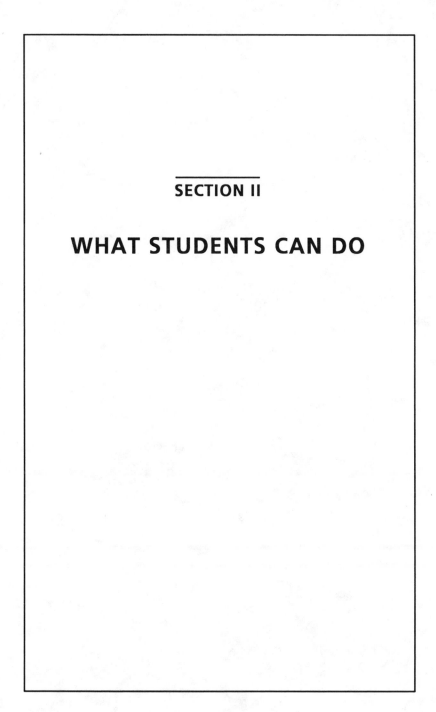

SECTION II

WHAT STUDENTS CAN DO

WHAT STUDENTS CAN DO

Making good grades involves two separate factors. One is obviously to score high on tests and assignments. The other involves what might be called "administrative factors." We'll explain both of these factors.

THE STUDENT'S ROLE IN ACADEMICS

We'll start with something that's often overlooked because it's so obvious: Hand in all assignments, and hand them in on time. One reason for this is that even a couple of zeros will have a devastating effect on your overall average. For example, suppose a certain subject involves four assignments. Student "A" hands them all in on time and gets an 80 on each. Average grade: 80. Student "B" hands in three of the assignments — again getting 80's on all three — but fails to turn in the fourth. Average grade for Student "B" is a 60. One missed assignment out of four cuts the average grade by 20 points!

For the same reason, handing in assignments late usually hurts your grade since most teachers will only give partial credit for late work. You have to do the same amount of work either way, so why lose points just by turning in the assignment late? (Of course, it's a lot worse to not hand in an assignment at all and get a zero.)

MANAGING YOUR TIME AND YOURSELF

The most important key to developing good study habit is time management. To be a success at anything, you must learn to use your time to the best advantage. If you manage your time wisely, you will have time to study, you will make good grades, and you will still have time for your friends and recreation.

The key to time management is scheduling study time every day so that you will have time to complete all assignments and will not have to cram for tests. Once you have made your schedule, stick to it. You will find that a good schedule is one of the best study tools. You will be surprised at how much improvement you can make simply by budgeting your time more wisely.

Your parents may help you to develop a schedule, but time management is your responsibility. No one can tell you what is the best schedule for yourself. Only you know which subjects you need to spend the most time on during the week. Develop a schedule that is right for you. Time management can be an important part of your growth as a person. It will help you develop habits of self-discipline and self-reliance that you will use all your life.

There are three important elements in planning your study time:

1. Know when to study.
2. Know where to study.
3. Know what to study.

Use these elements to make a daily study schedule. Once your schedule is complete, it will save you the time of deciding what to do and when to do it.

The first few weeks will be the hardest when learning to work on a schedule. However, when you become accustomed to a schedule, you will find that it takes away some of the pressures of studying. A well-developed and full schedule will put you in command of your studies.

An important factor in your success at school is how you spend your time after classes. Often these hours include scheduled activities such as athletics, extra lessons, housekeeping chores, or a job. It is up to you to schedule study time around your outside activities. Study time must be a priority.

You should study as soon after school as possible while the subject is still fresh on your mind. If you cannot find time for studying, you may find it necessary to cut back on outside activities. However, with a carefully planned schedule, you should have plenty of time for both study and extracurricular activities.

The following are suggestions of how to plan your study schedule:

1. Plan to study the same subjects at the same time each day. Doing this prepares you mentally to concentrate on that subject at that time. This kind of concentration is like physical exercise. The more you work at it, the easier it becomes.

2. Plan for emergencies and special events. Be ready to make adjustments in your schedule to include time for them. It helps to include an occasional free period in your schedule to make up for study time lost to some emergency.

3. Break your study time into 15-minute blocks to take advantage of your span of concentration. At the end of each block, test yourself over what

you have studied. This method will break your study time into manageable chunks.

4. Remember that the quality of your study time is more important than the amount of time you spend. If you are well organized, you can study more profitably in half the time you used to spend. Stick to your study schedule and use each time period wisely.

5. Plan ahead for daily and weekly review sessions, as well as additional review time before a quiz or test.

6. Besides a daily time schedule, prepare a long-range schedule that includes important events like term papers and special reports. Planning for these projects will help you keep to your schedule. Remember, your schedule is not a strait jacket to keep you tied down: A flexible and realistic schedule sets ample time for study, recreation, socialization, and relaxation.

Once you have followed your new schedule for a couple of weeks, you won't want to do without it. You will find that you have fewer worries about deadlines and falling behind, more time for personal interests, and better grades. Well-used time is like money in the bank that keeps drawing interest every day.

Where to study

It is important to have a specific place set aside for studying. It may be a corner in your room or a separate room. Wherever your study place is, it should be set up for work and concentration only. There should be no television, stereo, headphones, or other distractions. During your study time, you should not have visitors, phone calls, and/or interruptions. Soon you will develop the habit of concentrating in your own study area.

In choosing a study area, think about comfort and efficiency. The room should have the right temperature and lighting. If the room is too warm, you may get sleepy. If it is too chilly, you will be uncomfortable and unable to concentrate. Keep the temperature around 70° F. for peak alertness. The lighting in your study area should be indirect or diffused lighting. Lights that are too bright can cause eye strain.

Arrange your study area so that you have everything you need from the start. You should have several sharpened pencils, plenty of paper, and other items you might need such as rulers or protractors. Keep a dictionary, a thesaurus, and other reference book within reach. Don't allow missing materials to provide you with an excuse to leave your study area and break your concentration.

When you have finished studying, always put everything back the way it was when you started. That will save you time the next time you start to study. Make sure your homework assignments are in the front cover of your notebook.

What to study

To get the most out of your study time, structure your assignments from each class. Most of your assignments will consist of some kind of problem solving. Define the problem that you need to solve. This will give you a goal for your studying.

If you do not have a specific assignment to work on, work ahead. Do a chapter survey on the next chapter. Review your notes from the text and from lectures. Study ahead for tests you know are coming up. Learn all vocabulary words. Try to locate patterns in information from chapter to chapter. In social sciences, it is particularly helpful if you can find trends from one historical period to another. Social studies teachers like test questions and assignments that compare time periods or trends in history. English teachers like comparisons between different kinds of literature. Looking for links in a chain will not only impress your teacher, it will help you understand the material you read.

In completing an assignment, do the following:

1. Make a preliminary survey. Look for the purpose of the assignment. Develop a plan of attack with a specific goal.
2. Summarize what you have learned. Relate this knowledge to things you have learned in previous assignments.
3. Keep up with your work in each class. You must turn in all assignments in order to get an average grade. You must put forth extra effort for above average grades. You cannot make high grades if your assignments are missing, late, or incomplete.

Summary

Time management is the key to developing good study habits.A carefully arranged schedule is one of the best study tools you have. Studying and reviewing a certain amount each day will keep you from falling behind in your work and having to cram for tests. Review is the key to long-term memory, which is the key to making high scores on tests. Time management is also a good way to learn self-discipline and self-reliance.

The three important elements in planning study

time are knowing when to study, where to study, and what to study.

A daily schedule will help you plan and manage your time more wisely. You should schedule time to study every subject each day. You should study your hardest subjects first and spend more time on them.

Your study area should be quiet, well-lighted, and have no distractions. You area should have pencils, paper, and reference books within reach.

To get high grades, don't fall behind in your work. Turn in all assignments on time and put forth extra effort.

The following questions will help you manage your time. Answer each question on the lines provided.

1. If you do not have a specific course assignment, how can you spend your study time?

_____

_____

_____

2. Why can time management in school help you prepare for a career?

_____

_____

_____

3. What must be your first priority when putting together your schedule? _____

_____

_____

4. Why is it necessary to study at the same time and in the same place every day?

_____

_____

_____

5. What are five ways in which time management can help you improve your grades?

_____

_____

_____

_____

_____

ORGANIZATIONAL SKILLS

Just by organizing your school work in a certain way, you can cut the amount of time and effort needed to make any given grade by roughly two-thirds. (Or if you prefer, you can make much better grades without spending any more time and effort than you're spending now.) I'll tell you exactly HOW to do it in this section, but first I'd like to explain WHY organizing your school work is so effective.

Imagine that at the start of the school year, you are given a stack of note cards, each of which has one test question you'll see in the coming year, along with the answer to that question. With such an advantage, you probably wouldn't just go home and throw the whole stack into a big box. Instead, a clever student would probably sort the cards by course and topic, so that before any test, all you'd have to do would be to grab the dozen or so cards for that test and memorize the answers.

This is precisely the reason for organizing your school work, and the tool that makes it easy is a special type of notebook, with dividers for each class, and pockets in the covers.

Using the Notebook

Behind each divider, put your class assignment sheet. (See page 26.) This sheet lets you keep track of what topics were covered, what assignments are due, and when tests are scheduled in each class.

Each day, for each class, write down what you do in that class. Every class should have an entry for each day, even if the teacher does not give an assignment. These entries should be brief but detailed. For example, don't just write "read chapter;" state what chapter and what pages. This helps you keep track of what text material you are responsible for on the next test.

The pocket in the front cover of the notebook is for homework assignments that are ready to be handed in. Don't just slip homework inside the cover of your textbook because it can just as easily slip out again. If that happens, then when it's time to hand in your assignment, all you can say is "I REALLY did my homework, but I just can't find it right now." If you think that sounds pretty weak, you're right.

The back pocket of the notebook is for assignments that have already been graded and returned.

Getting ready for the "Dawn Launch"

When you've finished your homework for the evening, stack your notebook and school books in a convenient spot so they'll be ready for school the next day. You should put your books in the same place every night. This will help ensure that when you leave for school the next morning, you'll have everything you need.

GETTING THE "BIG PICTURE"

Have you ever wondered why some people can remember details better than others? Why can some people recall specific dates and events better than others? Are these people smarter than the average person? Do they have a better education? Not necessarily. They are simply people who understand the whole picture before breaking it down into parts.

Imagine you're in a contest to see who can put together a jigsaw puzzle in the shortest length of time. The winner of the contest gets $1,500,000 — the approximate amount of money you will make in a lifetime if you get a college education. Everybody will be putting together a similar puzzle and will start at the same time.

What would you say if I told you that you get to look at the picture of what the puzzle looks like when it is assembled, but the other people in the contest will not have that opportunity? It would probably make you very happy since you would undoubtedly win the $1,500,000. You would be able to assemble the puzzle much faster than those people who were not allowed to see the picture first.

So the first and most important thing you can do in any class is to GET THE BIG PICTURE. What type of information is going to be presented and in what order? The easy way to do this is to use two simple but powerful tools: book surveys and chapter surveys.

Book Surveys

On the first day of school, take a few minutes to survey the textbook. The word "survey" is defined as "To look at its entirety; to view in a general way." Answering the following book survey questions helps you get the big picture — what the authors expect you to know after you've finished the book.

A book survey includes the following:

1. What is the title of the book? The title of the book tells you in a few words what the whole

book is about. Does the book have a subtitle? For example, if you see that the complete title of your textbook is *American History: 1865 To Modern Times*, you have learned something important about the period of time that you will be studying. What would you expect to study if the title were, *American History: From The Pilgrims To Modern Times*? You would know that you would be learning about a much longer period of time in American history.

2. When was the book published? This can be very important since old books sometimes contain information that is no longer correct. For example, a book published before the Berlin Wall was torn down and Germany was reunited could not accurately describe Germany's present condition.

3. Table of Contents
   Examine the Table of Contents carefully since it is a detailed outline of the entire book. Examine the chapter titles and subtitles. As you do this, see if you can determine how each chapter is related to the other chapters in the book and how they are all related to the title. The relationship between chapters in a section often shows the order of importance the author places on events or the people involved in a particular time period. The test furnished by the same textbook company will follow the same pattern.

4. Preface or Introduction
   Read the Preface or Introduction. This will tell you in a page or two what the author expects you to know after you have studied the book. For example, imagine that you want to plant a garden. Would you dig up the earth with your

hands so that you could plant your seeds, or would you look around to see what tools were available to help you to dig holes? It wouldn't be smart to dig with your hands when there are tools in a nearby shed, would it? For the same reason, you look in the Preface to find out what tools are available in your book to help to "dig out" the important information in the text.

5. Index and Glossary
Look at the Index in the back of the book. The Index is a list of all subjects that are found in the book. It also gives you the page number where you can locate information about specific subjects. Knowing how to use an Index can reduce homework time.

Does the book have a Glossary? If it does, use the Glossary instead of a dictionary. The Glossary definitions usually will be the definitions that your teacher wants you to use in your homework (and know for the test.)

6. Unfamiliar Words
Look for unfamiliar words in the title and the Table of Contents. Look them up in a dictionary or the Glossary in the textbook and write their definitions.

7. General Impression
Thumb through the entire book in order to obtain a general impression of its content and layout. Try to discover whether the book is going to be easy to study or difficult to study. Books that include major and minor subtitles are often easier to study than books that do not. Books that have more than one color print are usually easier to study than books that only have black print. Some book

publishers will even make books easier to study by turning subtitles into questions.

The following exercise will help you to become more efficient in surveying textbooks.

A. Read the following information about a textbook. Then answer the questions by making a check mark in the blank beside each correct answer.

American Literature In The Twentieth Century by Dr. Eugene Phillips, American Literature Professor at Columbia University. Copyright 1988.

1. Judging from the title, what does this book contain?
   a. _____ an overview of American history
   b. _____ an overview of world history
   c. _____ an overview of twentieth century American literature
   d. _____ a detailed look at a few twentieth century American writers

2. Which of the following is NOT something you can tell about the author of the book?
   a. _____ where he teaches
   b. _____ what his name is
   c. _____ how old he is
   d. _____ what general subject he teaches

3. Which of the following books would be discussed in this literature textbook?
   a. _____ American novelist Nathaniel Hawthorne's *The Scarlet Letter* (1850)
   b. _____ British novelist Iris Murdoch's *Under the Nest* (1954)

75

c. _____ American novelist John Updike's *Rabbit, Run* (1960)

d. _____ American novelist Saul Bellow's *A Theft* (1989)

Answers: 1.c 2.c 3.c and d

B. Read each group of chapter section headings. Then read the list of chapter titles that follow. Circle the title of the chapter that would contain all of the section headings.

1. Measuring the length of an object
   Measuring the mass of an object
   Measuring the intensity of light
   a. Chemical Compounds
   b. Harnessing Energy
   c. Measurement in Science
   d. Experimenting with Sound

2. Pavlov and the conditioning of animals
   Social behavior of animals in groups
   Animals that defend territory
   a. Human Behavior
   b. Animal Behavior
   c. Plant Behavior
   d. The Nervous System

3. Acid rain
   Pollution in the Great Lakes
   Rebuilding the ozone layer
   a. Environment and Ecology
   b. Exploring the Solar System
   c. Meteorology
   d. The Polar Ice Caps

Answers: 1.c 2.b 3.a

Chapter Surveys

The chapter survey is the key that gives you an advance look at the information ahead. It lets you quickly and easily pull the most important information out of a textbook. It will put you ahead of the rest of the class, and more importantly, will let you know what to expect. You should do a chapter survey on every chapter that will be used on a test.

Timing is very important when doing a chapter survey. Whenever you have a test, you should do a chapter survey on the next chapter that night. For example, if you have a test over chapter three on Thursday, Thursday night you should do a survey over chapter four. This simple method will give you a major advantage over your classmates the next time the class meets since you will know what's about to be presented. You'll already have the big picture.

If the teacher skips around from chapter to chapter, simply ask the teacher what chapter will be covered next. Be sure to ask this on test day. Get in the habit of doing this as you finish each chapter.

The first six questions of a chapter survey take only about fifteen to twenty minutes to do. It is one of the best investments in study time you can make.

1. Title
What is the title of the chapter? The title will tell you in two or three words what the whole chapter is about.

2. Summary
Read the summary or review at the end of the chapter. Either of these will help you get "the big picture." You should read the summary first for the same reason a good carpenter looks at the plans for a house before he starts building it. If you pay close

attention to the information presented in the summary, you'll probably be able to predict many test questions.

3. Subtitles
On a sheet of notebook paper, list all major subtitles. Write them in the form of a question. Leave space (two or three lines) under the major subtitles and then list the minor subtitles. Also write the minor subtitles in the form of a question. You can turn any subtitle into a question simply by adding who, what, where, when, or how to the front of the statement. Often you might want to ask more than one question about a subtitle. For example, if the subtitle is the Battle of Bunker Hill, you might want to ask yourself: Who fought in the battle, where was it fought, when was it fought, why was it fought?

When you've completed this step, you'll have a skeleton outline of the entire chapter.

4. Relationships
While you're listing the major and minor subtitles, try to figure out how they are related to each other and how they are related to the title of the chapter.

Refer once more to the list of subtitles from the history textbook in the example. As the student looks at the outline, he should ask himself how each of the topics relate to each other or how they would be effected by each other. For example, do you think that you will find that the qualifications are different for membership in the House and Senate? Since there is a whole section devoted to Congress, do you think that it will be very important? By the time you have finished this part of the chapter survey, you will have a pretty good idea of what will be covered in the chapter.

5. Visual aids: Carefully examine all graphs and charts. They often present a large amount of information condensed into a small space. If you take a few minutes to examine graphs and charts, you will probably have a better understanding of the explanation that covers half of a page in your textbook.

A picture may be worth a thousand words, but do not spend a great deal of time studying contemporary photographs and illustrations. Photographs are often used to fill space and balance ratios such as ethnic groups or male/female balance.

If special feature pages are in the chapter, scan them. More than likely, no test questions will come from the special feature pages, but they are a good source for ideas for papers and extra credit work.

6. Definitions. Look up the definitions of all unfamiliar words in the title, chapter headings, and subtitles. Make sure you know the meaning of all the words in the vocabulary section at the end of the chapter.

The chapter survey outline works well for most subjects. I use a slightly different form for literature and math. The following examples show chapter surveys, book surveys, and surveys for literature and math.

A major purpose of the math survey is to get you to start working ahead, trying to solve the problems in the next day's lesson. Even if you can't solve a problem, at least you will be able to ask intelligent questions about the material introduced in the textbook.

BOOK SURVEY

Do a book survey on each of your textbooks. Answer the questions on the lines provided.

1. What is the title of the book?_____
2. Who is the author?_____
3. When was the book published?_____
4. Study the Table of Contents. Ask yourself how each chapter relates to the title and to other chapters.
5. Read the Introduction, Preface, or Foreword. What does the author want you to accomplish by reading this book?_____

_____

6. Get the General Impression. Rapidly scan the entire book to gather general impressions and main ideas. After scanning the book, write what you think is the main theme of the book.

_____

_____

_____

7. Index and Glossary. Look at the topics in the Index. Write five topics that are of special interest to you.

_____

_____

_____

8. Look for unfamiliar words in the title and Table of Contents. Look them up in a dictionary or in the Glossary and write their definitions.

_____

_____

CHAPTER SURVEY

Use the questions on this worksheet as a guide to doing a survey on each chapter you are assigned.

1. What is the title of the chapter? _____

_____

2. Read the Summary or Review at the end of the chapter. What are the main points of the chapter?

_____

_____

_____

3. On a separate sheet of paper list the major and minor section headings. Write them in the form of questions.

4. How do the section headings relate to each other? _____

_____

_____

_____

5. Examine all illustrations, photographs, charts, and graphs. Pay close attention to the charts and graphs.

6. Look up the definitions of all unfamiliar words in the title, chapter headings, subtitles, etc. Write them down.

7. Answer the questions to Number 3.

THE WAY TO AN "A"

LITERATURE SURVEY

1. What is the setting of the story? (time, place, season, etc.) _____

_____

_____

2. List the main characters and describe them.

_____

_____

3. Give a short summary of the story on a separate sheet of paper.

4. What is the conflict in the story? Is it internal or external? _____

_____

5. What is the theme?_____

_____

6. What is the point of view? _____

_____

_____

7. Look up definitions of all unfamiliar words in the story and write them down.

8. Make a plot curve to show the story line.

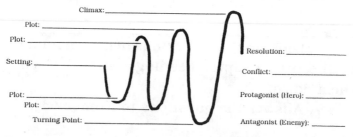

Everything that happens at the top of the plot curves is good for the protagonist (hero), and everything that happens at the bottom of the plot curves is bad for the protagonist (hero).

MATH SURVEY

Use the questions on this worksheet as a guide to doing a survey on each chapter you are assigned. Remember that it is important to do the survey before the teacher begins to explain it.

1. What is the title of the chapter?

_____

2. Read the summary or review at the end of the chapter. What types of problems will you study in this chapter? (Example: Multiplying and dividing fractions; quadratic equations; rules of exponents)

_____

_____

_____

_____

3. Definitions. Look up the definitions of all words and phrases that you do not know. For example, if you do not know what a "complex number" is, find out and write it down. _____

_____

_____

4. On a separate sheet of paper, write the major and minor section headings in the form of questions. (Example: If a major section heading is "Multiplication of Complex Numbers," you will write "How do you multiply complex numbers?") Leave 5 or 6 lines for the answers. In most text books the answers to your questions will appear in boxes and/or boldface print.

5. Using examples. On a separate sheet of paper, write down the example problems that your math book uses to explain or demonstrate the correct way in which to apply the formulas or methods that you wrote down when you did Part 4 of the survey. If there is more than one example, write out the last one. After following through the book's explanation of how to do the problem, try to do it yourself without looking at the book. If you can do the problem — including all of the steps — you will be ready for homework problems.

READING (HOW TO GET THE MAIN IDEA/ READING FOR COMPREHENSION)

After you have completed the chapter survey, the next step is to read the chapter. Students should read to answer the questions they have created in Step 3 of the chapter survey. When the student finds an answer to one of these questions, he or she should underline it lightly in pencil. Also underline bold face or italicized words with their definitions. (Remember to erase later if you haven't purchased the book.) If you aren't allowed to write in the textbook (even lightly), answer the questions on a separate sheet of notebook paper.

The most common mistake made by students is underlining too much in their texts. Every statement in your book is not important. Do not underline examples, explanations, transitions, or introductory material. Information of this kind is included to make the material go together as a story and make it interesting to read.

Reading to answer the questions not only teaches students how to get the most important information from a chapter, but also teaches reading comprehension. If you are having trouble understanding what you read, turn the subtitles into questions and then read to answer the questions.

The following exercise will help you become more proficient in getting the most important information from a textbook.

Read the following material. Underline the information in each section that you would consider most important.

Glaciers

A glacier is an enormous ice mass that moves over land. Glaciers are found in extremely cold areas such as polar regions. Glaciers form when fallen snow does not melt because of extreme cold. The snow slowly freezes into ice.

Kinds of Glaciers

There are two kinds of glaciers. The first is the *continental glacier*. These glaciers are huge, white sheets of ice that cover large areas of land. They completely cover the landscape, leaving no exposed land.

The second kind of glacier is the *valley glacier*. These glaciers are huge masses of ice that fill the valleys between mountains. They actually flow into the valley like water.

Glacier Movement

When they move, glaciers flow like water. Because of their great weight, they flow from high ground to low ground. The individual ice crystals that make up glaciers move over one another because of the pressure from the outside surfaces. This inside movement causes the entire glacier to move. A glacier also moves because the weight of the glacier puts pressure on its underside. The pressure causes heat, which melts the ice on the bottom of the glacier. The melting ice forms water, and the glacier slides forward on it. *Crevasses*, or large cracks in a glacier are caused when the glacier moves over uneven ground.

Land Changes

Glaciers change and reshape land as they move across its surface. One way a glacier changes land is by *eroding* the soil. Glaciers sometimes dig giant holes in the earth. A *cirque* is a round hollow cut into the side of a mountain. As a glacier moves toward or into a mountain, the ice *gouges out* huge amounts of dirt and rocks. Another kind of a gouged-out hole is created at the base of a mountain. If this kind of depression is below sea level and fills with sea water, it is called a *fiord*. Many fiords are found in Sweden and Finland.

Glaciers also deposit land formation as they move. One kind of deposit formation is a *moraine*. These appear as ridges consisting of sand, clay, and rocks and are located behind, beside, or in front of a glacier. Drumlins are small, rounded hills made of rock deposits. An *esker* is deposited by water that flows in a stream in a tunnel within a glacier. Eskers appear as narrow ridges of sand and gravel.

WHAT STUDENTS CAN DO

Use this worksheet to help you underline appropriate information in your texts.

1. Rewrite each section heading as a question.

_____

_____

_____

2. Find the information in each section that answers each question. Underline that information.

3. Write each boldface, italic, or colored word within the body of the test. Define each word.

_____

_____

_____

4. Double-check the information you did not underline. Be sure that examples, explanations, transitions, and introductions are not underlined. Did you underline anything that is not really necessary?

5. Did you miss anything that is really necessary?

NOTE-TAKING

Being able to take good notes is absolutely essential to efficient learning. Generally there are two sources from which you will take notes: your textbook, and your teacher. The reason for taking notes about things in your textbook is so you won't have to try to read everything again right before a test.

Taking notes from the things your teacher says is even more important because your notes are the only record you have of what the teacher thinks is important. If you miss an important point in your textbook, you can go back any time and reread, but if you miss a point in a lecture, it's gone forever!

The farther you go in education, the more important it is to learn how to take notes from a lecture. In college, most test questions come from the instructors' lectures and review sessions.

The Mechanics of Taking Notes

If you are a student who has just started junior high school or middle school, you might not know how to take notes. There are a few simple guidelines to follow that will make it easy for you to take good notes.

1. Name and Date.

Always put your name and the date at the top of your paper before starting. Doing this first means that you will never turn in homework and not get credit for it. Also, if notes happen to get out of your notebook, having the date on them will help you reassemble them in the order they belong.

2. One Side Only.

Make notes on only one side of your piece of

paper. It is easier to read notes if there is writing on only one side of the page. Also, you will sometimes need to use the back of the paper to write down the answers to questions you have about things that you did not understand.

3. Use Outline Form.

This is much more efficient than jamming everything into one big paragraph. An example of the outline form is given at the end of this chapter. One of the most important benefits of this method is that it helps you to understand what is important when you are reviewing.

4. Shorthand.

It is all right to use your own form of shorthand in your notes. For example, you might write "4" instead of "for". The important thing is that you understand what you wrote. See the list of standard abbreviations.

ABBREVIATIONS

Abbreviation	Meaning
E.G.	For example
N.B.	Note well; this is important
>	Greater than
<	Less than
=	Equals
/	Does not equal
[]	Important idea
?	Use in the margin to indicate that you don't understand an idea.
I.E.	that is
REF	Reference
ET AL.	And others
ETC.	Et cetera — and so forth

VS. . . . . Against
SQ. . . . . The following
Q.V. . . . . Which see (I.E., "Look it up")
EX . . . . Example

5. Neatness.

Even though these notes are for your personal use, keep them as neat as you can, simply because this lets you read what you've written.

Neat writing is much easier for both you and your teacher to read. In a test that was done recently, teachers were asked to grade an essay that a seventh-grade student had written. Some of the teachers received a neat copy of the essay and some teachers were given a messy copy. You will probably not be surprised to learn that the "neat" essay received much higher grades than the "messy" essay even though the content, spelling, and punctuation, were exactly the same.

6. Questions.

If you have questions about something that the teacher said or about something in the textbook, put a question mark in the margin of your piece of paper. As soon as possible, find out the answer to your question. When you do, replace the question mark with the answer. When you are reviewing your notes, you do not have to search for where you wrote down the answers to your questions.

Taking Notes from Textbooks

Reading a chapter in a textbook and then being able to pick out the most important information is a major problem for many students. If you sometimes get to the end of a chapter but do not know what you just read, do not get discouraged or think that you are not smart. You are not alone; there is a solution to the problem. When you are reading and underlining, what you are actually doing is trying to predict the questions that will be on tests. Isn't making a good grade on the test the main reason that you go to all this trouble of reading the material? Knowing what to underline and being able to predict what will be on a test is not too hard when you follow a few simple rules.

1. Use Chapter Surveys.

You will use the Chapter Surveys in your notebook to help you to take good notes from your textbook. Item #3 on the chapter survey tells you to turn the major and minor subtitles in your textbook into questions. You now read the material in the textbook in order to answer those questions. When you find the answer to a question, lightly underline it. Underline also words that are in bold print and italicized words, along with their meanings. Do not underline examples, explanations, transitions, or introductory material. Information of this kind is included to make the material flow together and to make it more interesting to read.

2. Write Down Your Notes.

Many schools do not allow students to underline in textbooks, even though the student may promise to erase the light underlining at a later date. That is not a problem. On the separate piece of paper on which you wrote down the questions, you left two or three blank lines between questions. When you find the answers to the questions you wrote down, write them down on those blank lines.

The following exercise will help you take better notes from a textbook. Underline the important points then complete the worksheet.

Thomas Jefferson helped Dolley Madison become known as a hostess. Madison, born in 1768, was married to Jefferson's secretary of state, James Madison. Since Jefferson's wife had died before he became president, he asked Dolley Madison to serve as hostess at official functions at the White House. She might have been especially sympathetic to Jefferson because she had been a widow when she married Madison. Dolley Madison became so popular with the people of Washington and with the rest of the country that people even began copying her clothing styles.

Dolley Madison's popularity increased when her husband followed Thomas Jefferson as president of the United States. Dolley Madison gave even more elaborate parties and entertainments than she had for Jefferson. She introduced new foods, such as ice cream, at special dinners. During the War of 1812, Dolley Madison became even more popular when she escaped from Washington just before it was captured by the British. She left behind some of her personal possessions so she could save such valuable items as the famous Gilbert Stuart painting of George Washington. President Madison won a huge majority of the vote for re-election in part because of his wife's popularity and also because the Federalist Party collapsed after protesting the war's necessity.

Practice taking notes from a textbook by completing the following outline.

I. _____

_____

   A. _____
   B. _____
   C. _____
II. _____

_____

   A. _____
   B. _____
   C. _____

Taking Notes From Lectures:

Note-taking from lectures is similar to note-taking from textbooks. You don't have to underline everything in a textbook and you don't have to write down everything the teacher says — only the important things. The problem is, of course, to figure out what is important. The following are tips to help you to determine the important "stuff."

1. "First and Last"
Be sure that you get to class on time and don't leave early. Why? The teacher usually covers the most important topics at the beginning of the class when she introduces her lesson for the day and at the end of the class when she reviews the day's lesson.

2. Verbal Clue
The teacher gives you verbal clues to emphasize the importance of the information that he or she is talking about. If the teacher gives you the following

verbal clues, write down what she says:
- a) "This is important . . ."
- b) "Listen-up"
- c) "The main goals are . . ."
- d) "The main reason is . . ."
- e) "You need to remember this . . ."
- f) "This will be on the test . . ."

3. Nonverbal Clues.

Teachers also give nonverbal (silent) clues when they are lecturing. Nonverbal clues include the following:
- a) writing information on the board
- b) raising or lowering her voice
- c) moving closer to the students shows emphasis
- d) using the hands to "talk" or to show emphasis

4. Emphasizing the Textbook.

If the information you read in the book comes up in a lecture, write it down because that information is important. If the teacher gives you a page number so you can get more information on a topic, write it down. The more often you see or hear the information, the greater the chance this information will appear on a test or quiz.

5. Prereading.

The key to taking good notes from lectures is reading ahead. Reading ahead keeps you ahead of the game and gives you the competitive edge. Can you imagine what it would be like for a letter carrier to try to deliver the U.S. Mail if nobody put up a mailbox? It would be difficult, wouldn't it? Trying to understand what your teacher says about a subject if you haven't preread is also as difficult. Reading ahead lets you know what is about to be presented in class.

Do not take notes on the back of your paper. Use the backs of your lecture notes to fill in gaps on each page, or use the space to write down answers to questions you might have. You might fill in gaps by including some of the details from the text or by comparing your notes with those of someone else in the class.

THE WAY TO AN "A"

Figure #6: The Modified Outline Form

Subject of Lecture

Main Point #1
- Example illustrating a main point or a significant fact about this point.
- Set off these subpoints by indenting, using dashes

Main Point #2
- Information about Main Point #2
- Example concerning Main Point #2
- Detail about this example, such as
- Date, place, time, etc.

Main Point #3
- Information about Main Point #3
- There will seldom be more than three main points in one lecture.

Use the following worksheet to help you take notes from your teacher's lecture.

Note-Taking from Lectures

Name: _____

Date: _____

Subject: _____

Title of Lecture: _____

Main Points of Lecture:

1.

2.

3.

Vocabulary Words:

1.
2.
3.
4.
5.
6.

Possible Test Questions:

1.

2.

3.

What did the teacher want you to learn?

Use this worksheet as you take notes from lectures. As you become more and more proficient, this checklist will become less necessary.

Have you prepared by:

1. Surveying, taking notes on, summarizing, and reviewing each section of your textbook BEFORE class?

2. Reviewing text notes so that you can listen for new ideas to add to those collected from the text?

3. Reviewing printed handouts before the lecture?

Have you:

1. Identified the central theme of the lecture?

2. Listened for main ideas and supporting details?

3. Summarized the speaker's ideas in a few sentences or phrases?

4. Used signal words to identify important ideas?

5. Kept distracting thoughts out of the way by anticipating the speaker's next idea?

6. Underlined points from the text that the speaker emphasized in the lecture?

REVIEW (HOW TO STUDY FOR TESTS)

Most of the tests you will have in school will have one thing in common: They will all test what is called "long-term memory." Short-term memory is what you read or hear. Long-term memory is what you are tested over. The key to improving your long-term memory is consistent review. In order to perform well on tests, it is important to review your notes everyday. Use the time you have set aside for specific subjects to review your notes in that subject. It is a much, much better use of time to study 15 or 20 minutes per day, five times per week, than to study for two hours the night before the test. Students will not only remember details and information better, but they will also remember it longer.

Some courses will be lecture-intense. In these courses most of your test questions will come from your lecture notes. In a class that is lecture-intense, you will have several pages of lecture notes. Instead of trying to learn everything in your notes, treat them as your text and highlight or underline the most important information.

Reviewing Class Notes

Taking notes from lectures is just as important as taking notes from a text. Students must review the notes every day. Timing is most important here. To best review notes from lectures, get to class a little early. While the teacher is waiting for the rest of the class to get there and while she is calling roll, you should be reviewing your notes from the previous class day.

When class is over, you should review the notes you took from class that day before you leave the class while they are fresh in your mind. If you have any questions over the material, you should ask the teacher at this time. This immediate review is another way to improve your memory.

Changing the Order of Review

Research has shown that people usually remember the first and last thing they hear or read. To prevent gaps in your memory, you should change the order in which you review your notes and other material for each class. Begin reading your notes at a different place each day. In this way you will be seeing different material first and last. For example, one day you might begin reading one-half of the way through your notes, read to the end, and then go back to the beginning and read up to the one-third point where you started.

Consistent daily review will keep you from having to cram for tests. Not having to cram for tests will mean that you will probably have more time for other things you enjoy while still scoring high on tests.

Consistent review is the key to turning short-term memory into long-term memory. Daily review of notes from textbooks and lectures will provide excellent preparation for tests and quizzes.

Answer the following questions about immediate review:

1. Why is it necessary to review immediately after class?

_____

_____

Answer: Immediate is a good way to lock information in the long-term memory bank.

2. How can you review if you have a class immedi-

ately following the one you just finished? _____

_____

Answer: Review during the break.

3. How long should an immediate review take?

_____

Answer: No more than five minutes.

4. What kinds of tasks should you do in an immediate review?

_____

_____

Answer: Review the notes you took that day. Ask the teacher to clarify information you do not understannd.

5. What can you do if you have eight pages of lecture notes per class hour for one class?

_____

_____

Answer: Underline or highlight your notes like you do in the note-taking from books.

6. If you have a class that is lecture-intense, what must you emphasize in all your reviews?

_____

Answer: Immediate review.

Use the following steps to help you understand what you must do in daily review sessions:

1. Which of the notes that you took today are main ideas that might be included on a test?

_____

2. What information from your survey of the text or other books helps explain what you studied today in class?

_____

_____

_____

3. What are the meanings of terms that were unfamiliar to you in today's work?

_____

_____

_____

4. After 20 or 30 minutes, take a five-minute break, then continue until all of today's notes have been reviewed.

Answer the following questions about reviewing for a test:

1. How can you assure yourself of having long-term memory?

_____

_____

Answer: By reviewing consistently.

2. What are two steps you should do for daily review?

_____

_____

Answer: Review immediately after taking notes consistently everyday.

3. How can you build your long-term memory for all the material that you have to review?

Answer: By reviewing the material every night.

4. What will happen if you do not review daily for each class that you take?

   _____

   _____

   Answer: You will have to study longer the night before the test.

5. How will daily review benefit you in taking tests?

   _____

   _____

   Answer: You will not have to cram the night before the test and you will retain the information longer.

Use these steps to help you understand what you must do in daily review sessions and in sessions before a test.

1. What ideas in this week's notes could be underlined as those so important they could be included on a test?

   _____

   _____

2. What ideas in the text or other books are so important they could be included in a test?

   _____

   _____

3. To highlight the ideas from books you could write them in the margins of your notes or if you

own these books, you can underline the ideas in the books themselves.

_____

_____

4. Write this information as questions you might see on a test.

_____

_____

5. Review for 20 to 30 minutes followed by five-minute breaks, and then continue reviewing.

TEST-TAKING

Performing well on tests does not come naturally to many students. Even students who really do know the material covered on the test may not do very well. Their problem is a mental one; it is called "test-phobia," or the fear of taking tests.

The treatment for any kind of phobia begins with informing or educating the person with the fear about the specific thing that they dread. In this chapter you will learn about tests. We will teach you how to eliminate test anxiety, how to predict test questions, how to study for tests, and how to take different types of tests.

Test Anxiety: The main cause of test anxiety is not being properly prepared. However, if you have followed the above procedure correctly, you will be ready to take any test that your teacher can give you. If you've been following the steps we've outlined in this book, you've been surveying each chapter, outlining or taking notes on the material, and reviewing the material regularly — at least fifteen minutes each day per subject. You've also spent at least five minutes per subject per day reviewing the notes you took in class. If you've done these things and if you apply the suggestions presented here, you will have all the information you need to pass the test.

Predict Test Questions: Knowing the questions that will be on the test is another way to eliminate test anxiety. This does not mean that you should try to sneak a look at the test ahead of time. Rather, you will predict for yourself what questions will be on the test.

Predicting test questions is very simple. In both secondary school and elementary school, most test questions come from the text book. (In college, more questions are based on the instructor's lectures.) Some of these questions are often the same ones you've created by rephrasing the subtitles in your textbook in the form of questions!

Many times teachers will tell you what will be on the test. Listen carefully when the teacher reviews for the test and take scrupulous notes. (See section on note-taking.)

Key phrases to listen for:

"This is very important."
"There will be a question about this on the
  test."
"These are the kinds of problems you will
  need to be able to solve in order to score
  high on the test."
"Be sure to review this well."
"Don't let this information confuse you."

When a teacher makes these kinds of statements in his/her class, be sure to indicate in your notes the information will probably be on the test. Do this by writing T.Q. (test question) next to the information.

The very best way to find out what information will appear on the test is to ask the person who is writing the test, the teacher, to help you study.

If you feel that you might do poorly on a test or if you are having trouble understanding a certain concept, make an appointment with the teacher to get extra help. Most teachers come to school early or stay late to help students.

When you are making the appointment, ask the teacher if you can come in before class or after class for extra help preparing for the test. Make sure you have specific questions to ask. Don't just walk in and expect the teacher to tell you what will be on the test.

After the test, make an appointment to talk to the teacher about what questions you missed on the test. Ask your teacher what you can do next time in order to be better prepared for future tests.

Many times when students are having trouble with a course, the trouble is not with the course material but with the teacher/student relationship. When the teacher is part of the problem, then let the teacher be part of the solution. The more time you spend with the teacher getting extra help, the more that teacher has invested in you. The teacher is going to want his/her investment of time and effort to pay off. The pay off is higher grades for you.

How to Use Your Textbook to Predict Test Questions

Students who know how to study and analyze a textbook will be able to quickly and easily predict test questions that come from the book.

1. Lists of learner outcome or information students should know after they have studied the chapter. If the textbooks give a list of learner outcomes or student objectives, make sure you have mastered that material.

2. Subtitles or subheadings. The subtitles that you changed into questions on Step #3 of the chapter survey will often become test questions.

3. Important terms. Textbooks often list important terms or vocabulary words at the end of the chapter. Important words may also be in bold face type or italicized or printed in a different color such as red or blue.

4. Lists of important points. When your text-book gives lists of important information, make sure you master the information.

Other Hints

Dates, Famous People, Places and Events

Teachers are not going to ask a lot of dates on tests, nor are they going to want you to list all the generals in WWI or when all the battles took place or where they were fought, but they will probably ask some questions like these. So how can you predict dates, famous people, places and events test questions?

The more times you see a date or proper noun in the text or in the notes you take from the teacher's lectures, the better the chances are that you will see the same information on the test. For example, if you see Philadelphia in the introduction to the chapter, within the chapter, and in the chapter summary, you will probably see it on the test. The same is true of dates and events.

Talk with students who have already taken the tests. Former students who have previously taken the tests and scored high on them can often give you valuable information on what you study. Often they are willing to explain strategies they used to get a good grade on the test. Teachers sometimes change test questions, but they rarely change their testing methods from year to year.

Examine old tests your teacher has given. Some teachers give students tests to keep, and some schools even have files of old tests.

By studying old tests, students often learn if a teacher takes most of the questions from the book or from lectures. You can also better predict the length of the test and types of questions. If a teacher's test consisted mainly of multiple choice and short-answer questions last year, chances are that he or she will follow the same format this year. Again, questions often change, but the format of the test usually does not.

Learn to predict test questions by paying close attention to class lectures and test reviews, learning how to study and analyze textbooks, talking with students who have taken the tests, and by examining old tests. The following exercise will help you predict test questions.

The most common types of questions are true/false, multiple choice, fill in the blank, and matching. Later, we'll show you strategies for answering each type of question.

The words in your text that appear in bold print and the vocabulary words at the end of the chapter will often appear in the form of "matching" questions, where you match each word in a column with its definition in the next column.

Studying for Finals

Study Blocks

When you study for finals, use study blocks to help you to cover a lot of material in a short amount of time. This study method is especially good for comprehensive finals. Most people can concentrate on one particular information block for only fifteen to twenty minutes at a time. Study blocks are designed to allow you to concentrate for an acceptable span and then relax.

To begin, divide the material you need to cover into blocks that can be covered in no more than twenty minutes. Make sure that each block is complete and is not just a block of information that does not relate to anything else. Define your blocks before you begin to study. A typical block may be anywhere from one page long in a Science textbook to five pages in a Social Studies text. To make sure that each study block is a complete unit, try giving it a title. If you can't give a block a title, you probably haven't divided the material appropriately.

As you study, try to find patterns within your material. Check for root words and prefixes or suffixes. Work with a pencil in hand because writing down key concepts helps embed them in your memory. Classify information and compare or contrast it to other bodies of information.

Approach each block to master it during the study time you've allotted. Do not count on coming back to an individual block at another time. At the end of your block of time, test yourself in writing over the material you have covered. If you do not do well on your own test, repeat the study block.

As an example of how to define study blocks, let us say that your biology class has been learning about frogs. When you are studying for the test on "Parts of the Frog," you decide to use study blocks. Rather than trying to review everything at once, you divide the material into three study blocks:

1. The Eyeball (Something your
   teacher emphasized)
2. Frog Muscles
3. Frog Bones

When you complete your study block on "The Eyeball," you will test yourself by turning the title into a question and then answering it. Your own personal test then becomes, "What are the parts of the frog's eyeball?" If you can write down all of the parts correctly, you are ready to move on to another study block.

Use the following check list to help you define and use study blocks:

1. Make sure the block you defined will not take more that fifteen minutes to cover.
2. Make sure the block can be studied as an independent unit.
3. Title your block. If you cannot give it a title, the block you have chosen is not an independent unit.
4. Look for patterns within the material that will help you remember what you have studied.
5. With unfamiliar words, look for familiar root words and affixes.
6. Classify facts within your study block. Compare and contrast the information in each block to the information in other blocks around it.
7. Test yourself over the information in your study block.
8 If you have not mastered the information, do the study block again.

Answer the following questions about studying for final exams:

1. If you have not reviewed and must cram for finals, what can you do to pass your tests?

_____
_____
_____

Answer: Make sure you have done a chapter survey on all chapters and know your vocabulary words.

2. Why is it best to use study blocks when studying for long periods of time?

_____

_____

Answer: Study blocks divide the material into manageable pieces of information. It also is more efficient since we know the mind works most effectively in blocks of 15 minutes.

3. How do you determine material to be covered in one block?

_____

_____

Answer: If you can turn the title into a question.

4. What are some methods you can use to fix information in your memory?

_____

_____

_____

Answer: Consistent review (review everyday) immediate review getting the big picture.

5. What can you do to determine whether you have covered the material in the study block and mastered it?

_____

_____

Answer: Test yourself by turning the title into a question and answering the question.

Use the following check list to help you define and use study blocks.

1. Make sure the block you defined will not take more than fifteen or twenty minutes to cover.

2. Make sure that the block can be studied as an independent whole.

3. Title your block. If you cannot give it a title, the block you have chosen is not an independent unit, and you should select again.

4. Look for patterns within the material that will help you remember what you have studied.

5. With unfamiliar words, look for familiar root words and affixes. Study and memorize diagrams and tables within the text.

6. Classify facts within your study block. Compare and contrast the information in each block to the information in other blocks around it.

7. Test yourself over the information in your study block.

8. If you have not mastered the information, do the study block again.

General Test-taking Techniques and Strategies

1. Learn when your test will be early and plan your study schedule. Be sure to study a little each night. Remember, the key to changing short-term

memory, what you hear or read, into long-term memory is consistent review.

2. Eliminate test anxiety. Being overprepared for tests is the best way to eliminate test anxiety. Anxiety can also be reduced by deep breathing and positive thinking.

3. Read directions and follow them. Students often lose points on tests simply because they do not read and follow instructions. How discouraging to know the answer to a question and miss it simply because you did not follow instructions.

4. Plan how much time to spend on each section of the test. Know how many minutes you have to complete the test. You should also pay close attention to the number and types of questions you must answer. For example, essay questions will take longer to answer than true and false questions.

5. Answer the easy questions first. This will build confidence and momentum. This will also help eliminate anxiety. You may also get clues from other questions that will help you answer the more difficult questions you do not know.

6. Answer all the questions. Even if you do not know the answer, do not leave the question blank. After you have learned the following techniques in this book, you will become more test wise. When you have to guess, the odds of guessing correctly will be in your favor.

7. Check your answers. After you have completed the test, go back and check your answers to make sure you have not made any careless mistakes. When checking multiple choice or true and

false questions, do not change your answer unless you are certain that it is incorrect. Studies show that your first guess is usually correct.

Now that you have studied for your test at least an hour, (not counting the time you spent doing your chapter survey or reading and outlining your chapter), and now that you know what is going to be on the test, you don't have to worry. By applying the above techniques, you will be able to answer the large majority of questions on most tests.

But you may ask, "What will I do if there is a question that I don't know the answer to, or what if my teacher throws in a trick question and I have to guess?" The following sections will teach you how to be test-wise, how to guess on tests, and how to increase your chances of guessing the correct answer.

Tests: General Information.

There are basically two different types of tests: short-answer and essay. We will first learn about the things that you want to do on all tests, and then we will learn about the best way to take specific kinds of tests. The things that you should keep in mind when you take any test are as follows:

1. Read the directions and circle what you are supposed to do.

Reading the directions for a test is absolutely essential. You do not want to miss getting credit for things that you know simply because you did not write down the answers in the form that was required.

2. Plan your time.

Take a few minutes before you begin a test to figure out how much time you should spend on each question. For example, if there are sixty questions to be answered in sixty minutes, you know that you have one minute per question. Do not spend so much time on one question that you do not have time to complete the test.

3. Answer easy questions first.

It is a good idea to answer the easiest questions first. You can return later to the more difficult questions. Sometimes you will find clues to answers within other questions.

4. Answer all questions.

Very few teachers deduct points for answers that are not correct. If you do have to guess, follow the hints about guessing that you will learn in this step.

5. Don't let "patterns" bother you.

Have you ever been bothered on a test by the fact that all of the answers were "True?" Sometimes you will have the same answer five or six times in a row, or the same pattern will be repeated. For example, the answers in a multiple choice test might be, "A, B, C, D, A, B, C, D . . ." Do not let patterns of answers bother you. Answer each question without worrying about patterns.

True/False Tests

The first type of short-answer test that we want to learn about is the "True/False" test. You will have the opportunity to practice what you learn about True/False tests.

"Practice" tests are included at the end of this chapter. You can increase your chances of doing well on a True/False test by keeping the following things in mind:

1. Assume a statement is true unless you can prove that it is false. There are usually more true answers than false answers on tests. After you have gotten into the habit of reviewing your notes on a regular basis, you will find that your instincts will help you to "prove" that a statement is false.

2. When reasons are stated, answers tend to be false. The clue words to look for are: the reason, because, since, due to." Example: T F "Rover is a dog because he has four legs." The answer is false because lots of animals other than dogs have four legs. (In this case, "Rover" happens to be a cat.)

3. Absolute statements tend to be false. Statements that do not allow for the proverbial "Exception to the Rule" tend to be false. Among the clue words that tell you that exceptions are not allowed are: no, always, not, never, everybody, nobody, best, always, all. Can you think of others? Example: T F "All cats have tails." The answer is false because a few species of cats − like the Manx − do not have tails.

4. Statements containing qualifiers ("Weasel words") tend to be true. A "Weasel Word" is a word that allows for exceptions to a rule. Some of these qualifying words are: many, frequently, most, few, seldom, usually, some, often, tend to. Can you think of others? Example: T F "Most cats have tails." The answer to this question is true. By substituting the word "most" for the word "all," we allowed for exceptions.

5. Longer answers tend to be true; shorter an-

swers tend to be false. Questions that are much longer than average tend to be true because it takes more words to make a statement true than it takes to make it false.

6. For the answer to be "True," all parts of the question must be true. Some students become confused when they find an answer that is partly true. Have some faith in yourself — if you see that a statement is even partly false, answer "False" immediately.

7. Restating false questions. Occasionally, you will be asked to restate false questions so that they are true. If you are asked to do this, look for qualifiers. Change absolute words to "weasel words" or find the word that does not fit and change it. Example: T F "All soldiers carry guns." Rewritten as a true statement: "Most soldiers carry guns." You can practice using your knowledge about True/False tests by taking the "fun" tests at the end of this chapter.

Multiple-Choice Tests

A multiple-choice question has three parts: the stem, options, and distracters. The question is called the stem and the choices of answers are called the options. Distracters are answer choices that are "way out" — obviously not correct. You can increase your chances of getting correct answers on multiple-choice tests by remembering a few hints.

1. Eliminate the distracters. On most tests, two of the four choices are distracters. After you cross them out, you have at least a 50-50 chance of getting the right answer.

2. Absolute options tend to be wrong. If a choice does not allow for exceptions, it is not likely to be the correct answer.

3. In tests over material you have studied, unfamiliar-looking terms or phrases tend to be wrong. Because you are reviewing your lecture notes and textbook notes every day, the right choice will almost certainly be something that sounds familiar to you.

4. More complete or inclusive options tend to be correct.

5. "All of the above" is usually a good guess.

6. Similar options. When two options are similar in appearance, the correct answer is often one of the two.

7. Use True/False strategy. Turn the choices you have NOT eliminated into True/False questions. If you can answer "True" to one of these statements, then the answer is correct.

8. Pick the "Best" Answer. Many times you will be asked to pick the "Best" of several correct answers. If you are directed to do this, always select the most specific answer.

Matching Questions

Matching questions are another kind of short-answer question. It is a good idea to sort answers into categories. An example, your categories may be: people, dates, places, things. Mark out the answers as you use them. Examine the sample test at the end of this chapter in order to see how this should be done.

Completion or Fill-in-the-Blank Questions

In completion or fill-in-the-blank questions, look for clues within each question to help with the answers. Look for spaces left blank. Does the length of the line vary? If it does, the line length will be a clue to the answer. The answers will usually be a definable term, so study the vocabulary words for each chapter.

Fill-in-the-blank questions are often used to test your knowledge of terms or vocabulary. Very often the answers for this type of question will come from the vocabulary at the end of a chapter in your textbook. Remember that those words are also the words which appear most often in bold-faced print in the textbook. Look for clues within the questions.

Essay Questions

Essay questions are different from short-answer questions because the answers must be at least one paragraph long. Read the directions for essay questions carefully. The terms "explain, describe, compare, discuss, define, and contrast" do not mean the same thing. Determine what the question is asking you to do before you begin formulating an answer.

Answer every part of an essay question. Many essay questions have more than one part.

Example: List the causes of the American Revolution. Compare them to the causes of the French Revolution. Discuss the governments that followed each revolution.

This question has three parts. Failure to answer completely any one of these parts might mean a failing grade for the entire question.

Organize your answers. Before you begin writing the answer to an essay question, plan what the major points will be and list them on a separate sheet of paper. As you write, make sure that your writing style is clear and that your major points are clearly stated.

Write as if the person reading it knows nothing about the subject, and it is your duty to inform and teach that person. Write more than you need to write in order to answer the question. Before you turn in the answer to an essay question, proofread it. Make sure that all your statements are complete and that you have no sentence fragments. If you run out of time, outline the main points of your answer and request that the teacher allow time for you to finish writing it. Most teachers understand.

This list of ten steps will help you in writing for an essary test answer or in constructing a writing assignment given as homework.

1. Read all questions.

2. Do the easiest first. This helps one thought lead to another and the whole picture comes into focus which will help bring the other answers to mind.

3. Organize the information before writing the answer to make sure the information is stated as the question requires.

4. Use writing skills learned from English classes to write the best answer. Start with an introductory sentence or paragraph that has a topic sentence or thesis statement which identifies *what* is being written and *how* the information will be given.

    A. Use comparison or contrast for example when writing about periods in history or how two or more things were discovered in a science break-through.

B. Use order of importance to write about the significance of something. Think of examples for each. The most important may be either first or last, but follow an order. State the order and be sure to identify the most important.

C. Use chronological order when the information is a step process or has a definite relationship to events in history.

5. Conclude the answer with a summary sentence or paragraph.

6. Write neatly and use good grammar. Incorrect spelling can cost points because teachers aren't mind readers.

7. When in doubt expound on what you know by using your facts as comparisons or analogies.

8. If you run our of time or have poor writing skills, use an outline method of listing the main points with supporting facts. This is better than nothing.

9. Very rarely can a teacher be fooled by "padded" answers. A large number of random words will often reduce points rather than add points.

10. If there are other types of answers, answer them first. The information may help you get ideas of organization or help you get missing facts for the essay questions.

The following exercises will help you become better at taking tests. Read each step below. Then follow the directions in each step to answer the questions.

1. Circle the signal words in the statements below. Mark X beside the statement that gives a general rule that applies to most, but not all, cases. Then mark O beside the statement that applies to all cases.

_____ a. Most presidents of the United States re-tire from public life after completing their terms of office.

—— b. No president has ever led a branch of government after the end of his term in office.

Answers: a. X — most b. O — No

To determine which statement in #1 is true and which is false, it is necessary to check them against the facts of various presidents' lives.

2. Read the following facts. Then write answers to the questions.

Fact: Dwight D. Eisenhower served two terms as president, retired to Kansas, and wrote memoirs of his public life.
  a. Did Eisenhower serve in political office after his term as president? _____
  b. Does this fact seem to make the statements in #1 true or false? _____

Answer: a. no b. true

Fact: After serving as president, William Howard Taft was appointed chief justice of the Supreme Court.
  a. What office did Taft hold after presidency?
  _____
  b. Which statement in #1 is true? ——————
  c. Which statement in #1 is false? ——————
  d. What part of this statement tells you that it is false?

Answer: a. Chief Justice of the Supreme Court
b. "a" c. "b" d. No president has led a branch of government after ending his term of office.

123

3. Now look at the following multiple choice questions about the presidents. The facts from #1 and #2 can help you determine that two of the choices are incorrect. Draw lines through these two choices.

Question: Which president served in Congress after completing his term in office?
 a. Dwight D. Eisenhower b. James Garfield
 c. Andrew Johnson   d. William Howard Taft

4. To determine which of the two remaining choices in #3 is correct, it is necessary to check them against the facts of various presidents' lives. Read the following facts. Then write answers to the questions.
 Fact: William Henry Harrison, Abraham Lincoln, James Garfield, William McKinley, Warren G Harding, Franklin D. Roosevelt, and John F. Kennedy all died before completing their terms as president.
 a. What does the question in #3 want to know?
_____

 b. Which of the remaining choices in #3 died before completing his term in office?
_____

 c. What is the correct choice to the question?
_____

 Answer: a. Which president served in Congress after he was president. b. Garfield c. "c"

5. Use the facts from #1 through #4 to match the presidents with the facts about them. Use the process of elimination to find the answer for the president who was not discussed.

Presidents	Facts
___ Dwight D. Eisenhower	a. served in Congress after his term as pres.
___ William Howard Taft	b. also served as chief justice of the Supreme Court
___ Theodore Roosevelt	c. wrote memoirs about his public life
___ Andrew Johnson	d. became president upon William McKinley's death
___ James Garfield	e. died before the end of his term as president

Answer: c b d a e

6. Answer the following questions to locate the basic information you might need to answer an essay question about Taft's career in public life. Mark NA beside questions that cannot be answered by examining the facts in #1 through #5.

a. Who would the answer be about? _____
b. What did he do in public life? _____
c. When did he join the Supreme Court? _____
d. Where did he complete his work? _____
e. Why was his career unusual? _____

f. How did he achieve these offices? _____

Answer: a. Taft b. He was president of the U.S. and then he served as Chief Justice of the Supreme Court. c. After he was president. d. in Washington e. He was the only president to have done this. f. NA

7. If you find that you have not covered all the details necessary to write a complete essay answer, it might still be possible to make a good grade by relying on information that might already be in your memory. Answer the following questions.

    a. Which questions in #6 could not be answered with the facts in #1 through #5?

    b. In what city do the U.S. Congress, the president, and the Supreme Court conduct their daily business?

    c. How do people become president of the United States or chief justice of the Supreme Court?

Answer: a. "f" b. Washington, D.C. c. They are elected or appointed.

Mark T beside each true statement and F beside each false statement. Circle the part of the false statements that make them false.

_____ 1. Nothing will replace regularly scheduled reviews in preparing for tests.

_____ 2. Fear and carelessness cause more mistakes on tests than any other factors, according to research.

_____ 3. Read all directions twice and underline key words.

_____ 4. The first questions to answer are the ones that you are not sure about.

_____ 5. Pace yourself by scheduling equal amounts of time to answer each question.

Answer: 1.F 2.T 3.T 4.F 5.T

Read each question and the four choices for each. Circle the letter of the choice that answers the questions or completes it.

8. Which of the following is NOT an item you would find on an objective test?

a. true/false   c. essay question
b. multiple choice   d. matching

Answer: c

9. Short statements on true/false tests may tend to be:

a. true   b. factual   c. false   d. complete

Answer: a

10. To help you narrow down the choices on multiple choice tests, you should:
a. draw lines through choices you know are incorrect.
b. assume that the first and last choices are incorrect
c. assume that the second and third choices are incorrect
d. mark your first hunch.

Answer: a

11. How might later items on a multiple choice test help you answer questions you are unsure about?

a. They might help you relax and concentrate.
b. They might give you clues to the correct answer.
c. They might reword the question in a way you will understand.
d. They might tell the page in your text where the answer was explained.

Answer: b

12. How can you discover answers to matching items you are unsure about?

   a. by rereading other sections of the test for clues
   b. through the use of the 5W's and the H
   c. by skimming the information in the definitions
   d. through the process of elimination

   Answer: d

13. Which of the following is NOT a technique to be used in answering essay questions?

   a. emphasizing what you know best
   b. giving your own opinion and drawing your own conclusions
   c. using broad terms and backing your statements with details
   d. keeping your answers brief since the teacher already knows the answer

   Answer: d

14. When writing essay questions answers,

   a. leave out diagrams or pictures because they do not show your understanding of the subject.
   b. make a list that answers the 5W's and the H.
   c. do not cause confusion with your ideas by including statistics.
   d. leave out examples so that your answer is short and concise.

   Answer: d

Match the terms with their definitions.

_____ 13. reviewing

a. include such items as true and false, multiple choice, and matching

_____ 14. objective tests

b. require written, detailed explanations an answers

_____ 15. essay tests

c. gives you the background you need to do well on a test by helping you retain the main ideas of your material

Answer: 13.c 14.a 15.b

More Practice Tests: True/False

Directions: Read all questions carefully. Put an X over the correct answer. Circle the clue words or phrases.

T F 1. By the year 2000, the number of Americans over the age of 65 is predicted to be greater than the number of Americans under the age of 25.

T F 2. Seventh-grade students always dance better than eighth-grade students.

T F 3. The reason so many people own dogs is that dogs are more friendly than cats.

T F 4. The number of lawyers in the United States is growing faster than the population.

T F 5. Australia is a popular place to go for vacations because it is cheap to fly there.

T F 6. Canadians live longer than Americans due

to the fact that Canada has a colder climate.

T F 7. Students who are polite to their teachers usually get better grades than rude students.

T F 8. The Berlin Wall was torn down because it was old and beginning to crumble.

T F 9. Technological change usually precedes social change.

T F 10. There are at least eight thousand people in the United States who are over 100 years old.

T F 11. Most people under the age of six do not like to eat Brussels sprouts because they look like little cabbages.

T F 12. Everyone who makes straight A's has an I.Q. over 110.

T F 13. All high school athletes want to become professionals some day.

T F 14. Colleges usually do not offer remedial English courses because most high school graduates do not need them.

Answers: 1.T 2.F 3.F 4.T 5.F 6.F 7.T 8.F 9.T 10.T 11.F 12.F 13.F 14.F

Practice Test: True/False

Directions: Read questions carefully before answering. Write the word "True" or the word "False" in the space to the left of the numbers. Circle the clue words or phrases.

_____ 1. All of the states of the Confederacy seceded from the Union in the same year.

_____ 2. Everybody plays Nintendo for six hours a day.

_____ 3. The main purpose of taking World History is to learn how to sound intelligent.

_____ 4. Employees invariably prefer the reward of recognition for work well done to the reward of getting a raise.

_____ 5. Employees sometimes prefer the reward of recognition for work well done to the reward of getting a raise.

_____ 6. Most teachers really do like their students.

_____ 7. Getting a high school diploma is important if a person wants to get a good job.

_____ 8. All immigrants to the United States came because they wanted religious freedom.

_____ 9. The reason America was not discovered until 1492 is that everyone thought that the world was flat.

_____ 10. Baseball is the favorite sport of all true Americans.

_____ 11. Parents are always the people who are

best qualified to teach their children how to drive.

_____ 12. Taking tests can be fun sometimes.

_____ 13. Everyone should go to college.

_____ 14. Turning in assignments on time is not important because teachers will always grade them later.

_____ 15. Students who have good study skills usually get good grades.

Answers: 1.F 2.F 3.F 4.F 5.T 6.T 7.T 8.F 9.F 10.F 11.F 12.T 13.F 14.F 15.T

WHAT STUDENTS CAN DO

Practice Test: Matching

Directions: Match the items in the list on the right with the items in the list on the left. Use each item in the list on the right only once.

1. The fear of heights

2. Occupations of the Scottish

3. Language spoken by Brazilians

4. American Indian population

5. Century America discovered

6. First President to be assassinated

7. Teenage "hangout"

8. Social problem of early settlers of the west

9. Nation of first modern industrialization

10. Occupation of Mauri people

a. 1,000,000

b. Abraham Lincoln

c. Video arcade

d. Mining and farming

e. Shortage of women

f. England

g. Acrophobia

h. Fifteenth

i. Hunting

j. Portugese

Grouping Answers
(You will see how much easier the test is once you have grouped the possible answers!)

<u>People</u>	<u>Places</u>
Lincoln	England
Portuguese	Video arcade

<u>Numbers</u>	<u>Things</u>
Fifteenth	Shortage of women
1,000,000	Hunting
	Mining and farming
	Acrophobia

Answers: 1.g 2.d 3.j 4.a 5.h 6.b 7.c 8.e 9.f 10.i

THE ADMINISTRATIVE WAY
OF MAKING GOOD GRADES

THE ADMINISTRATIVE WAY
OF MAKING GOOD GRADES

Until now I've been discussing ways to improve your "academic performance" — your scores on tests and homework assignments. But there's another factor in getting good grades that few people know about. It involves getting "the system" (mainly teachers) to work to your benefit. You could consider it a kind of "psychological warfare" designed to make the teacher believe that you deserve a better grade.

We call this method the "administrative way" of making good grades, and it is highly effective. Here's how to get better grades the administrative way.

Don't be tardy or miss class.

Being on time for class shows consideration for the teacher. Also, since the beginning of the lecture often contains an overview of the material to be covered, it's one of the most important parts. Missing this vital information makes it much harder to get "the big picture."

Obviously, you can't expect to make good grades if you don't attend class! Even if you make up your class work, many test question come from information obtained during class. If you absolutely MUST miss class, ask your parents to write the teacher a note explaining why you were absent. Be sure to ask the teacher to let you know about any assignments or important announcements you missed.

If you MUST miss a class, your number one task when you return is to ask the teacher what assignments were made while you were out. Make sure you turn in any missed assignments promptly. Making up assignments is crucial not only to your grade, but also to getting the teacher on your team.

Get the teacher on your team.

It is very important to get the teacher on your team because the teacher is the scorekeeper, and virtually every teacher occasionally gives an extra point or two at the end of a grading period to students who have obviously made an unusual effort, have good attitudes, have turned in all their papers on time, and so on.

Be sure to thank teachers for going above and beyond the call of duty to help you. Many teachers spend long hours before and after school helping students. A thank-you card or a Christmas or Valentine card with a special note telling the teacher that you are aware of the extra effort she has put forth to help you be successful in his/her class will make you stand out in the teacher's mind.

Some students might think that this is playing up to the teacher," but all you're really doing is just showing good manners and class (pun intended)."

"Position Yourself for Success"

We put this in quotes because it's a cliche in the business world, but in the classroom it's LITERALLY true: You'll get better grades if you position yourself in the "power seats." The power seats are the seats on the front row. Studies have shown that most teachers teach to the front and to the right (the teacher's right), so students in those areas get more help from the teacher.

Students at Harvard Law School know this and take full advantage of it. When part of the final grade is based on student participation, students often camp out on the door steps the night before the first class to make sure they get the power seats.

Sitting in the front of the room also helps you stay focused on the subject rather than on passing notes to your friends. (There's time enough for that after class.) So if possible, get a seat at the front of the room on the teacher's right.

Don't become a "discipline problem."

Behavior is usually a good indicator of how well a student will do in class. Students with good grades usually have good behavior, and vice versa. This is so well known that teachers sometimes unconsciously use it as a PREDICTOR of academic performance!

More to the point, teachers remember the students who give them a hard time. If you're a problem for the teacher, you can't expect to get what might be a badly-needed "grace point" come report card day. And sometimes ONE POINT can make the difference between an A and a B (or passing and failing).

Make friends with students who usually make high grades.

Don't become friends with students who drive teachers to distraction. People judge you by the company you keep.Become involved in class discussion.

A teacher often will give extra credit for regular class participation.

Extra Credit

You should regard all extra credit possibilities as mandatory. If the teacher doesn't announce that extra credit work is possible, ask about it anyway. Often teachers give credit for correcting a paper with a low score. You may even be able to get a few points of extra effort by doing the chapter survey and outline discussed earlier!

Timing

Timing is important when asking for extra credit. Don't wait until the day before report cards come out to ask for extra credit. Extra credit is the insurance policy that will insure that you reach your grade goal.

Improving Grades

If you have done badly on a test, show your teacher your preparation for study, your chapter survey, and your lecture notes. Tell your teacher how you reviewed your notes everyday. Ask for ways that you can improve your grade in the future. Point out that you have worked to make a good grade but have not accomplished your goal. Ask for help to improve your grade and reach your grade goal.

Summary:

Success in school is not necessarily related to I.Q. Using the administrative way of making good grades will help you be competitive for the top grades. The administrative way of getting good grades includes:

1. Being present and punctual to all classes.
2. Getting the teacher on your team.
3. Positioning yourself for success.
4. Not being a discipline problem.
5. Making friends with people who are good students.
6. Taking part in class discussion.
7. Taking advantage of all extra credit.
8. Getting the teacher to help you if you are not reaching your grade goal.

Conclusion

The way to an "A" is a cooperative effort. Teachers record grades and use a mathematical table to turn grade averages into letter grades or pass / fail reports. Parents provide the time to study and a quiet place to study. Students use the ability to read in study and preparation for class. When all three components complete their designated tasks, there is the satisfaction of success. The unique requirement is that all three must work together .

This work may be seen in the comparison of three horses pulling a heavy load up a hill. When one horse does not pull a third of the load, the other two horses will grow weary of the additional burden. Can you imagine how much greater would be their strain in trying to carry the load if the third horse simply lay down and refused to move, or if the horse turned to go down hill because it was easier than to go up hill. The horses have to cooperate to move the load. The teacher, the student, and the parents will enjoy seeing the effort of cooperative work produce an "A" on the report cards.

Logic dictates that it is in the teachers' best interest to have high test scores from their classes.

Any adult who returns to the schoolroom for a full day of observation usually sees teachers who are truly concerned about students' needs. When the teachers have the opportunity to work as a team with the student and the parents, they are more often than not willing and cooperative. You have a positive attitude to win them to your team. However, if by chance, you meet the one teacher who has forgotten that desire to help students, you have the steps to remedy the situation.

Students are learners; they don't have all of the answers yet. They learn best by example. They learn to speak the language they hear. They learn to act as they see others react. They are young enough, creative enough, and energetic enough to take the world as it is and move forward. Thank goodness they have the innocence to try to solve the world's problems, the dream of being better off on their own, and the audacity to question the status quo. They will learn how to use this study plan in order to master the current system or change it. They are too bright to refuse the tools they need to rise above the level where low grades have placed them. These students know who holds the keys to the car, the house, and the money to afford an easier life style. The parent has the key ring and the authority by law to guard those keys.

The key to total success is by statute in your hands. As a parent or legal guardian, you have the steps to win cooperation from the educational system, you have the time-management and organizational plan to guide your child to academic success, and you have the desire to help your child. You know to send your child to school prepared to learn. Students can do this best when fed, dressed, and encouraged to have a good day. Schools feed, dress, and counsel the disadvantaged child because the experts in physical development have found this is important to the overall ability to learn. You have seen that the physical needs of your child were met. Now you are providing for your child's academic need. You have bought into this program. All that is left for you to do is plan the success celebration you and your child have earned.

BIBLIOGRAPHY

Chubb, John, and Toby Chubb. *Politics Markets And American Schools*. Washington, D.C.: The Brookings Institution, 1990.

Des Jardins, Charlotte. *How To Get Services By Being Assertive*. Chicago: Coordinating Council For Handicapped Children, 1985.

Firth, Terry. *Secrets Parents Should Know About Public School*. New York: Simon and Schuster, 1985.

Nemko, Dr. Marty, and Dr. Barbara Nemko. *Private School Education In A Public School*. Washington, D.C.: Acropolis Books, 1986.

Peters, Tom, and Robert H. Waterman, Jr. *In Search Of Excellence*. New York: Warner Books, 1982.

Popham, James W. *Advising Schools: A Handbook For Concerned Citizens*. Los Angles: Instructional Objectives Exchange, 1977.

Rioux, William. *You Can Improve Your Child's School*. New York: Simon and Schuster, 1980.

ABOUT THE AUTHOR

Jan Barrick began her teaching career in 1973. Since that time she has taught students with learning disabilities, educable mentally handicapped, and students identified as being gifted and/or talented. She has taught students in elementary school through college as well as planned and implemented teacher training programs and training programs for parents. She has earned a bachelor's and a master's degree in education from the University of Oklahoma.

In 1988, she opened Alpha Plus Learning Centers. These centers were designed to help students improve their grade point averages and become more successful in school. The Alpha Plus method is now used in several school districts to help students improve their school performance.

ORDER INFORMATION

THE WAY TO AN "A"

For additional copies of *The Way to an "A"*, telephone TOLL FREE 1-800-356-9315. Master/VISA Card accepted.

To order directly from the publisher, send your check or money order to Rainbow Books, Inc., Order Dept., P. O. Box 430, Highland City, FL 33846-0430.

Book/Video Cassette: $29.95 plus $4.00 shipping and handling ($33.95 postpaid).
Book: $12.95 plus $3.00 s/h ($15.95 postpaid).
Video: $14.95 plus $3.00 s/h ($17.95 postpaid).

For QUANTITY PURCHASES, telephone Rainbow Books, Inc., 813-648-4420 or write to the publisher, Rainbow Books, Inc., P. O. Box 430 Highland City, FL 33846-0430.

If your school is interested in adopting the Alpha Plus Study Skills Program, please call or write:
Alpha Plus Systems, Inc.
1207 W. Main
Norman, OK 73069
405-364-4024